Andy Seed

THE SILLY BOOK OF Weird AND WACKY WORDS

Illustrated by
Scott Garrett

To Sam and Megan

Published 2015 by Bloomsbury Publishing Plc
50 Bedford Square, London, WC1B 3DP
www.bloomsbury.com

Bloomsbury is a registered trademark of Bloomsbury Publishing Plc

ISBN 978-1-4088-5338-2

Copyright © 2015 Bloomsbury Publishing Plc
Text © 2015 Andy Seed
Illustrations © 2015 Scott Garrett
Additional illustrations © Shutterstock

A CIP record for this book is available from the British Library.

Printed and bound in Great Britain by CPI Group (UK) Ltd, Croydon CR0 4YY

1 3 5 7 9 10 8 6 4 2

IMPORTANT:
The author and publisher recommend enabling
SafeSearch when using the Internet in conjunction
with this book. We can accept no responsibility for
information published on the Internet.

CONTENTS

INTRODUCTION

Some people play with footballs, some people play with cards, some people play with their food and some people (the best people) play with words. Wordplay involves all sorts of things: jokes, poems, puns, riddles, making up phrases, messing around with spellings, twisting people's tongues and thinking of comical names – and much more than that too.

The important thing about wordplay is that it's FUN. This book has more words in it than you can fit on the bulbous belly of a blue whale: it has absolutely oodles, preposterous piles, ludicrous lashings, stonking stacks of the stuff, including wordplay games to try. It's all here, ready for you to enjoy – what are you waiting for?

JUICY JOKES AND RIDDLES

Everybody loves a good joke and many of the best jokes use wordplay to make us chortle. But don't worry, there are none of those dreadful 'dad puns' here, just clever wit, cheeky riddles, new takes on old favourites and lots of loopy lines to leave you laughing.

One-liners

One-liners are short jokes that often fool around with language. Unlike many jokes, they don't use the Q&A format.

I didn't use to finish sentences, but now I

I just let my mind wander, and it didn't come back.

You can't have everything; where would you put it?

I heard about a man whose whole left side was cut off but he's all right now.

Police station toilet stolen – the cops have nothing to go on.

Archaeologist: someone whose career lies in ruins.

It's bad luck to be superstitious.

I'm going to get to school on time, no matter how long it takes!

Wildlife wit

Animals are a favourite topic for jokes – well, they can't answer back, can they? Enjoy these:

What looks like half a camel? The other half.

Why do cats chase birds? For a lark.

What do you get if you cross a cat and a gorilla? An animal that puts *you* out at night.

What do you get if you cross a Crocodile and a hyena? I don't know but I'll join in if it laughs.

Why did the whale cross the road? To get to the other tide.

What did the spider say to the bee?
Your honey or your life.

When does a duck go 'moo'?
When it's learning a new language.

What do you get if you cross an elephant with a skunk?
Rid of it.

What's the best way to keep milk from turning sour?
Leave it inside the cow.

SWAG

HONEY

Bumper stickers

Bumper stickers are funny slogans stuck on the back of cars and trucks. Often they are something to do with driving but sometimes they are just short jokes.

Follow that car, Godzilla - and step on it!

Sorry for driving so close in front of you.

Of all the things I've lost,
I miss my mind the most.

Rock is dead. Long live paper and scissors.

Honk if you see parts fall off.

Don't use shampoo
– demand real poo.

Corduroy pillows are
making headlines.

GRAVITY ALWAYS GETS ME DOWN.

Money is the root of all evil –
for more info send me £5.

No one is listening
until you fart.

He who laughs
last thinks
slowest.

11

Riddles to untwiddle

Can you work out
the solution to
these natty riddles?

1.
What can you catch
but not throw?

2.
What has a
neck but no
head?

3.
What has a face and
two hands but no
arms or legs?

4.
What can you
hold but not
touch?

5.
What has to be
broken before
you can use it?

6.
What is it that, after
you take away the
whole, some still
remains?

7.
What kind of tree
can you carry in
your hand?

8.
What five-letter
word becomes
shorter when you
add two letters
to it?

Answers on p156.

Brain-ache riddles

These word puzzles are harder than the previous ones.
Maybe try them out on a handy adult...

1.
What begins with T, ends with T and has T in it?

2.
What loses its head in the morning but gets it back at night?

3.
What goes around the world but stays in a corner?

4.
What is so delicate that even saying its name breaks it?

5.
What's tall when it's young and short when it's old?

8.
What are always fast, next to last, never there, everywhere?

6.
What can run but never walks, has a mouth but never talks, has a head but never weeps, has a bed but never sleeps?

7.
You must use it to change it. If you lose it you're out of it. What is it?

Answers on p156.

Nutty riddles

These riddles are silly, but fun too. How many can you get?

1. What word begins and ends with an 'e' but only has one letter?

2. What type of cheese is made backwards?

3. Which letter of the alphabet has the most water?

4. What starts with a 'P', ends with an 'E' and has thousands of letters?

5. Forwards it's heavy but backwards it's not. What is it?

6. What kind of coat can only be put on when wet?

7. Can you name two days starting with T besides Tuesday and Thursday?

8. If you take four eggs from nine eggs, how many do you have?

9. Where does yesterday follow today, with tomorrow between them?

Answers on p156.

14

Top notch knock knocks

Sometimes the old ones are the best.
And sometimes they are the worst...

Knock knock.
Who's there?
Tank.
Tank who?
You're welcome.

Knock knock.
Who's there?
Cook.
Cook who?
That's the first one
I've heard this year.

Knock knock.
Who's there?
Yoda Lady.
Yoda Lady who?
I didn't know you
could yodel.

Knock knock.
Who's there?
Howard.
Howard who?
Howard I know?

Knock knock
Who's there?
Toodle.
Toodle who?
But I've only
just arrived!

New ones

And here are some new knock knock jokes...

Knock knock.
Who's there?
Want.
Want who?
...three, four, who's that
knocking at my door?

Knock knock.
Who's there?
Nasty.
Nasty who?
SHOCK!

Knock knock.
Who's there?
What's up.
What's up who?
Well, it's brown and smelly.

Knock knock.
Who's there?
Banana.
Banana who?
Knock knock.
Who's there?
Banana.
Banana who?
Knock knock.
Who's there?
Banana.
Banana who?
Knock knock.
Who's there?
Orange.
Orange who?
Orange you glad I
didn't say 'banana'?

Doctor, Doctor!

These medical jokes have been around for ages but new ones are being invented all the time.

Arrrrrr!

Doctor, doctor I think I'm a pirate.
OK, open your mouth and say, 'Arrrrrr'.

Doctor, doctor my daughter has swallowed a pen, what should I do?
No need to worry madam, just use a pencil.

Doctor, doctor, I only have thirty seconds to live.
I'll be with you in a minute.

Doctor, doctor, I broke my leg in two places.
Well, stay away from both of them.

Doctor, doctor, I swallowed a fish bone.
Are you choking?
No, I really did!

Doctor, doctor I've swallowed a tape measure.
How long has it been in there?
About 20cm.

Doctor, doctor, I can't stop stealing things.
Have you taken anything for it?

What do you call a man...

Name wordplay is always good for a laugh and these puntastic little jokes are particularly fun because many of them are guessable.

What do you call a man...

With a seagull on his head?	Cliff
With a fish on his head?	Rod
With a kilt on his head?	Scott
With a map on his head?	Miles
With a voice recorder on his head?	Mike
With a car number plate on his head?	Reg
With stolen goods on his head?	Rob (or Nick)
With a spear on his head?	Lance
With a ship on his head?	Nelson
With a tiger on his head?	Claude

What do you call a woman...

These are remarkably similar to the previous jokes.

What do you call a woman...

With a pond on her head?	Lily
With a glass ball on her head?	Crystal
With berries on her head?	Holly
With the sun on her head?	Dawn
With coins on her head?	Penny
With a kebab on her head?	Donna
With a book on her head?	Paige
With sausages on her head?	Barbie
With two toilets on her head?	Lulu
With John Terry on her head?	Chelsea

Wheely good

These jokes are fun to ask people.

What car does Tiger Woods drive? · A Golf

What car does a big cat drive? · A Jaguar

What car does a dog drive? · A Rover

What car does a well-dressed person drive? · A Smart Car

What car does an alien drive? · A Galaxy

What car does Charles I drive? · A Cavalier

What car does Paul McCartney drive? · A Beetle

What car does a saxophone player drive? · A Jazz

What car does someone who doesn't know the words drive? · A Hummer

Graffiti

A lot of graffiti is too rude, but here are some amusing examples of things written on walls.*

QUESTION EVERYTHING
WHY?

BEWARE OF THE DOG
HE IS VERY SARCASTIC

THE FIRST THREE MINUTES OF LIFE CAN BE THE MOST DANGEROUS the last 3 are pretty dodgy too...

Anyone interested in time travel meet me here last Thursday

DO YOU HAVE TROUBLE MAKING UP YOUR MIND?
WELL, YES AND NO

Always be sincere...even when you don't mean it

*Important: don't put graffiti on walls yourself!

Q&A puns

Puns are the kind of word jokes that dads or grandads like. Some dad-puns are so bad that the police may have to issue a warning. These, however, are good (you'll be policed to know).

⊙ Q: What's a bear's favourite pasta?
A: Tagliateddy

✪ Q: Why did the cat sleep under the car?
A: Because it wanted to wake up oily.

⊙ Q: What did the bee trapped in an oven say?
A: Swarm!

✪ Q: If buttercups are yellow, what colour are hiccups?
A: Burple.

⊙ Q: Which of King Arthur's knights invented the round table?
A: Sir Cumference.

✪ Q: What's white, light and sugary and swings from trees?
A: A meringue-utan.

⊙ Q: What did one shooting star say to the other?
A: Nice to meteor.

✪ Q: How many eggs does it take to make a stink bomb?
A: A phew.

Punorama

See if you can make up some like these:

*

I used to have a fear of hurdles, but I got over it.

*

A man drowned in a bowl of muesli. He was pulled
under by a strong currant.

*

I was going to look for my missing watch but
I couldn't find the time.

*

When a clock is hungry it goes back four seconds.

*

Beethoven and Mozart will never be forgotten,
even now they're decomposing.

*

It was a very moving wedding – even the cake was in tiers.

*

Don't be scared of aardvarks – a little aardvark
never hurt anyone.

*

I've never seen a man-eating tiger but
I've seen a woman eating chicken.

Commercial comedy

Shops, cafés and businesses love having
punny names. Here are some of the best.

Prints Charming Art seller

A Salt and Battery Fish and chip shop

Ryan Hair Barbers

Bits and PCs Computer repair

Thai Tanic Restaurant

Planet of the Crepes Pancake van

Sure Lock Homes Locksmiths

Lord of the Fries Fish and chip shop

Sofa So Good Furniture store

Florist Gump Flower seller

Wok this Way Chinese Restaurant

Chisel Me Timbers Joiners

Lesser-known songs

Sadly these were never hits...

'My Car's the Best' by Scott Everything

'Our Love is Gone' by Gladys Over

'Grill It, Baby' by Chris P. Bacon

'Can't Stop Staring' by Hugh Jize

'Gone Fishin' by Courtney Thing

'Smell the Morning' by Norma Snostrils

'Itching for You' by Ed Lyce

'Falling for Pat' by Rhoda Cow

'Little, Green and Famous' by V.I. Pea

'You Gotta Be Positive' by Ken Do

'New Country' by Bertha Furnation

'A Place to Live' by Bill Jerome Holmes

'Where's That Picture?' By Sonia Fone

WEIRD WORDS AND FUNNY PHRASES

According to the people who write the Oxford Dictionaries, there are at least 250,000 words in the English language. That's a lot, in case you didn't spot it. Some of them are ordinary ('cup'), some are long ('electroencephalography'), some are little-known ('ogdoad'), some are funny ('foozle') and some are new ('selfie'). Here are all sorts of interesting words and expressions.

Intriguing words beginning with Q

Some interesting words you might not know:

qigong a Chinese exercise routine, like tai chi

quaff to drink something with enjoyment

quagga an extinct yellowy-brown zebra

quiddity a distinctive feature of something or someone

quinquagenarian a person who is in his or her fifties

quokka a small wallaby which can climb trees

Five long words

There are some very long words in English, but not many. Here are five:

Archaeoastronomy (16 letters)
the study of what ancient people knew about space.

Cuprosklodowskite (17 letters)
a green radioactive mineral found in Africa.

Oversimplification (18 letters)
to explain something while missing out important details.

Incomprehensibility (19 letters)
not being able to understand something.

Counterrevolutionary (20 letters)
a person trying to stop a revolution.

Whatsits

Ever said, 'Pass me the thingamajig'? We've all done it! Here are some more
words for that item you've forgotten the name of.

whatchamacallit

doofer   doodah   whatsit

thingummy   thingamabob   oojamaflip   thingamajig

nicknack   thingy

A quotum of obsolete words

Obsolete words are no longer used, but they are still fun.
A quotum is a part, by the way.

Blottesque a blotchy style of painting

Cumsloosh a person who flatters someone

Derf bold or daring

Grimalkin a cat

Hallihoo lucky or holy hood for babies

Hurrock a heap of stones

Lunarian an inhabitant of the Moon

Nabble to gnaw something

Izzard the letter Z

Pelf money

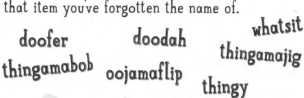

Hyphenated alphabet

Can you think of any more?

A-Team   Hilarious 80s TV show about a load of tough guys with a minibus

B-movie   A low budget 40s black & white film usually featuring a no good cowboy

C-cup   A bra size

D-day   June 6th 1944 when the Allies landed in Normandy during World War II

E-Type   A famous Jaguar sports car of the 60s/70s

F-Plan   A popular 80s diet: you were supposed to stuff yourself with baked potatoes

G-force   The force of gravity – multiplied on those monster theme park rides

H-bomb   Hydrogen bomb – a very nasty, powerful atomic weapon

J-Cloth   A disposable cleaning cloth

K-Tel   Music company that sold fab compilations via TV ads in the 70s

L-shaped   You know, as in L-shaped room and, er, other things

N-type A type of semiconductor used in electronics

O-Level The exams your dad used to do before GCSEs were invented

P-wave The fastest shockwave which travels away from an earthquake, of course

Q-Tips Those cotton bud things which you mustn't stick in your earholes

R-value A measure of insulation – the higher the better for lofts

S-Bend A bendy bend in the road – never take one at over 50 mph on your skates

T-Shirt Come on, everyone knows what a T-shirt is

U-Boat German submarine (short for unterseeboot)

W-X A diamond which has a light yellow colour

Y-fronts The classic large white underpant, sported by grandads and Homer Simpson

Z-Bed One of those folding beds which nearly takes your fingers off when you open it

Funny words

Why are some words funny? Nobody really knows! But, not everyone finds the same words funny, that's for sure. Here are some words that for some reason, quite a few people find amusing.

* gusset * pomp * underpants * eggy * bamboozle * monocle
* strudel * spasm * wibble * pooter * noggin

Annoying words

If people can't agree on which words are funny, then they really can't agree on which words are annoying. What irritates you word-wise? Maybe words that are used all the time like, er, like. Make your own annoying word list or ask your friends or family which words irritate them.

Some example from the author: **occidental, hashtag**

Silly words

Some words sound silly, others have a silly meaning or a silly spelling. Can you add to this list?

CAHOOTS – planning something with someone (in cahoots)

FLIBBERTIGIBBET – person who can't keep quiet or still

FROND – the leaf of a fern

GUBBINS – bits and pieces or stuff

GUTSY – brave

HEIRLOOM – a valued item passed on through a family over time

HIRSUTE – hairy

HOITY-TOITY – snobby or stuck up

KERFUFFLE – a fuss or commotion

NOUGAT – a chewy bar usually containing honey and nuts

PANTYHOSE – tights

PEEVE – to annoy

SKEDADDLE – to run away

TAUPE – a grey-brown colour

THWART – to spoil someone's plans

Here are some more to look up:

boffo   pzazz   eggbutt   snaffle

skosh   doofus   vamoose   wuss   ziti

They didn't have those when I were a lad...

New words are being made up and added to the language all of the time. Lots of them are connected with technology, but not all. Did you know that the words below were not even around 20 years ago?

app a digital programme for a portable device or computer

bezzie best friend

bling flashy jewellery or accessories

hipster an image-conscious young adult who values indie culture

hoody a hooded top

meh an expression showing a lack of interest

merch merchandise

onesie a loose, one-piece jump suit often worn for relaxing

retweet on Twitter, to share an existing tweet

sudoku a number puzzle based on a 9x9 grid

voicemail a system for storing phone messages

Zumba a dance-based exercise programme

Techno-babble

Because computer technology develops so quickly, new words to describe the latest developments are being invented all the time. Have you heard of these?

Bitcoin
a digital currency used to make payments online

cloud computing
using the internet to store and manage files

Google glass
digital specs that give the wearer an info display

kludge
a botched together, temporary computer program

netizen
a person who uses the internet regularly

phablet
a portable device sized between a smartphone and a tablet

ransomware
a virus that demands money in return for your documents

vlog
a video blog

zettabyte
a unit of information equal to 250 billion DVDs

Txt SSIF

(so stupid it's funny)

Text abbreviations are a kind of wordplay that have been around for a while but which are constantly developing. Here are some interesting ones:

10Q Thank you

2G2BT Too good to be true

AYMM Are you my mother?

BION Believe it or not

CWOT Complete waste of time

DUST Did you see that?

E123 Easy as one, two, three

HHOK Ha ha, only kidding

ICIHICPCL I can't imagine how I could possibly care less

LTHTT Laughing too hard to type

NIMY Never in a million years

ONNA Oh no, not again

POTATO Person over thirty acting twenty one

RRR Har har har

SLAP Sounds like a plan

TTFN ta ta for now

WACI What a cool idea

YOYO You're on your own

Lexi-con

Some people have fun making up silly words which are often combinations of existing words. See if you can work out where these came from:

Alpha mail a really strong envelope

Beaufart Scale system for measuring the power of trumps

Cavaleer to pull faces at Charles I

Courjet a very fast green vegetable

Gingerbred descended from red-heads

Mountainear what enables hills to listen

Nambypambee feeble insect

Non-friction really smooth books

Polar bare very cold arctic mammal

Queen's peach the monarch's favourite Christmas fruit

Reddy meal tomato soup

Shedule list of DIY jobs

Toilet role extremely poor part in a play

Wailbone sore rib

Nonsense words

Many writers have made up nonsense words over the years, often for comedy purposes. Here is a selection:

Jabberwocky

Lewis Carroll, wrote this famous nonsense poem as part of the 1871 book Through the Looking Glass, a sequel to Alice's Adventures in Wonderland. The poem contains many invented words including gyre, mimsy, vorpal and uffish.

Dr Seuss

The author the The Cat in the Hat and many other bestselling children's books, loved making up the names of new creatures such as the wocket, lorax, poozer and yekko.

Mary Poppins

The 1964 musical film Mary Poppins contains a famous song Supercalifragilisticexpialidocious. This invented word is supposed to mean 'something to say when you have nothing to say'.

Ken Dodd

Old school British comedian Ken Dodd is well known for his own special nonsense words including tattyfilarious, which doesn't really have a meaning but sounds funny.

The Simpsons

The legendary American TV series has featured many nonsense words over the years but the two most well-known are probably cromulent (meaning acceptable) and embiggen (meaning to grow) from 1996.

Blackadder

This popular UK TV series featured an episode about the writing of the first dictionary in which Rowan Atkinson's character annoys the book's author by mentioning a series of meaningless words including confibularities and frasmotic.

Sniglets

Sniglets are made-up words which are given a clear definition. They are the answer to a situation where no real word seems to exist – such as here:

 Blithwapping hammering a nail into a wall using an object that isn't a hammer, such as a shoe

Fraznit loose threads hanging from a jumper that cause it to unravel

 Lub a bit of spinach stuck between your teeth

Marp the hard-to-find end of a roll of sticky tape

Mostspur the annoying broken wheel on supermarket trolleys

 **FRAZNIT!**

Pulpid a young child who plays with the box more than the toy that was in it

Squatcho the button on top of a baseball cap

Woowad lumps of sticky rice served in Chinese restaurants

Sniglets are fun to make up. Why not create some of your own – or make up some other types of nonsense words?

Old news about oxymorons

An oxymoron is an expression made up of words that contradict each other or have the opposite meaning, for example:

Alone together	Deafening silence	Bitter sweet
Original copy	Instant classic	Seriously funny
Living dead	Awfully good	

Pleonasms from past history

A pleonasm is a piece of language that uses more words or parts than is strictly necessary. Can you see why these expressions fall into that category? A couple of them are also not regarded as proper words.

Kneel down	Tuna fish	Off of
Empty hole	Tiny speck	Bestest
Down south	Irregardless	Could possibly
Climb up	I didn't do nothing	

Horse idioms

The English language is full of sayings about cats, dogs and horses. This is what ten of the horse-based expressions mean:

A dark horse – someone who surprises people by revealing or doing something unexpected.

Get off your high horse – stop acting like you know better than other people.

Back the wrong horse – to support something or someone that cannot succeed.

Closing the stable door after the horse has bolted – to try and fix a situation when it's too late.

Don't look a gift horse in the mouth – to be ungrateful for something offered

Strong as a horse – to feel fit, well and strong

Get it straight from the horse's mouth – to find out about something from the person who knows most.

Flog a dead horse – to spend time on something when there is no point.

Horses for courses – what suits one person or thing might not suit another

You can lead a horse to water but you can't make it drink – you can give a person a chance to do something but you can't make him or her do it.

More beastly words

Animals have inspired all sorts of everyday phrases – do you know what all of these mean?

Bee-based sayings

- ✪ Buzz off
- ⊙ Stop droning on
- ✪ A bee in your bonnet
- ⊙ Honey, I'm home
- ✪ A hive of activity
- ⊙ sting in the tail

Cat-centric terms

- ✳ Cat nap
- ✳ Having kittens
- ✳ Has the cat got your tongue?
- ✳ Pussyfooting around
- ✳ Fat cat
- ✳ Let sleeping cats lie
- ✳ Copycat
- ✳ A cat among the pigeons
- ✳ The cat's whiskers

Old school exclamations

These are expressions of surprise that have been around for a long time.

Gosh!

Crikey!

By Jove!

I say!

Golly!

Gee-whizz!

Great scott!

Gadzooks!

Cripes!

Egad!

Heck!

My giddy aunt!

Tabloid speak

Some newspapers are very keen on using special phrases to mean certain things, especially in headlines.

Word	Meaning
Axe	cut
Blast	criticise
Outrage	anger
Plea	request
Probe	investigation
Rap	criticise
Riddle	mystery
Slam	condemn
Storm	row
Vow	promise

Estate agent speak

Estate agents sell houses and their brochures are well known for special phrases to describe the condition of homes. This list covers the full spectrum of conditions from the best to the worst.

1. Immaculate
2. Highly desirable
3. Charming family home
4. Well appointed
5. Period features
6. Deceptively spacious
7. Good decorative order
8. Compact
9. Realistically priced
10. In need of some modernization
11. Great potential for development
12. Requiring complete renovation

Classic film and comic clichés

In the past certain characters, both goodies and baddies, often relied on stock expressions in movies and cartoon strips. Here are some of the best.

'You won't get away that easily.'

'So, we meet again.'

'Take him away.'

'After them, quick!'

'Aren't you forgetting something?'

'You don't scare me...'

'It's a long shot, but....'

'Are you thinking what I'm thinking?'

'Silence, fool!'

'You'll never get away with this.'

'That's exactly what they want us to do.'

'Nothing can stop me now, mwah-a-ha!'

'You'll pay for this!'

'I, I can't hang on much longer.'

'Give me one reason not to kill you.'

'There has got to be a way out of here.'

TASTY TONGUE TWISTERS

Tongue twisters are horrid little expressions which we find difficult to say but which are is impossible to resist. We try them and we do okay when we go slowly but when we speed up... oh dear. They work by overloading the movements our mouths need to do to form different sounds.

Ones even your granny knows

Say these slowly at first then try to speed up:

> She sells sea-shells on the sea-shore
> Betty Botter bought a bit of butter
> Red lorry, yellow lorry
> Ed had edited it
> Chop shops stock chops

> Three free throws
> Sally Smith's Fish Sauce Shop
> The boot black bought the black boot back

Short ones

You have to repeat these at least four times:

→ Unique New York
→ Irish wristwatch
→ Flash message
→ Bad money, mad bunny

→ Greek grapes
→ Early oil
→ Mix, miss, mix

Try saying these fast

And repeating them. If you can, you're something special.

👉 Listen to the local yokel yodel

👉 Are our oars oak?

👉 The big black bug bled black blood

👉 Red leather, yellow leather

👉 Good blood, bad blood

👉 Is this your sister's sixth zither, sir?

👉 Fred fed Ted bread, and Ted fed Fred bread

👉 One smart fellow, he felt smart;
Two smart fellows, they felt smart; Three smart fellows, they all felt smart.

Hard to say at all

Even saying these once slowly is a challenge!

🌀 A bloke's back bike brake block broke.

🌀 Six thick thistle sticks

🌀 The Leith Police dismisseth us

🌀 Irish Wristwatch, Swiss Wristwatch

🌀 The sixth sick sheik's sixth sheep's sick.

🌀 The seething sea ceaseth and thus the seething sea sufficeth us.

Little rhymes to try

Some tongue-twisters come in the form of short verses. See
how you get on with saying these aloud.

One-One was a racehorse.
Two-Two was one, too.
When One-One won one race,
Two-Two won one, too.

How much wood would a woodchuck chuck
If a woodchuck could chuck wood?
He would chuck, he would, as much as he could,
And chuck as much wood as a woodchuck would
If a woodchuck could chuck wood.

Of all the felt I ever felt,
I never felt a piece of felt
which felt as fine as that felt felt,
when first I felt that felt hat's felt.

A tutor who tooted the flute,
Tried to tutor two tooters to toot.
Said the two to the tutor
'Is it tougher to toot,
Or to tutor two tooters to toot?'

49

Announcer's test

People who wanted to be radio presenters in the past would sometimes be given an announcer's test to see how clearly they could speak and whether they could manage to read a tricky passage without tripping up. Here is one from the 1920s for you to try and read aloud. A posh voice is essential.

Penelope Cholmondely raised her azure eyes from the crabbed scenario. She meandered among the congeries of her memoirs. There was the Kinetic Algernon, a choleric artificer of icons and triptychs, who wanted to write a trilogy. For years she had stifled her risibilities with dour moods. His asthma caused him to sough like the zephyrs among the tamarack.

How to pronounce some of the difficult words:

Cholmondely	chum-ley	triptychs	trip-ticks
azure	az-your	trilogy	trill-o-gee
scenario	sen-ar-ee-oh	risibilities	rize-ih-bill-ih-tiz
congeries	Con-jer-riz	dour	doo-er
cholerific	coll-er-riff-ick	sough	suff
artificer	art-ih-fiss-er	zephyrs	zeff-ers

Phrustrating frases

There are some words and phrases that many people find tricky to say properly. Watch out for these:

WORD/PHRASE	WHERE PEOPLE GO WRONG
Arctic	It has a c after the r: not 'artic'.
Athlete	Not 'oth-a-lete'
Espresso	There's no x: not 'expresso'
Et cetera	No x: not 'ex cetera'
Library	It has two Rs: not 'libary'
Luminous	Not 'illuminous'
Mischievous	Not 'mischiev-i-ous'
Phenomenon	It has 'nom' in the middle
Regularly	It is 'reg-u-lar-ly' not 'reg-u-ly'
Tenterhooks	Not 'tenderhooks'

Tongue-tripping places

The UK is full of towns, villages, castles and other places with names that you don't pronounce as they appear. I don't know who's responsible for this but it's really annoying and people have been known to giggle and point at those who get them wrong. So, here is your survival guide to Britain:

Place	How to say it
Alnwick	Annick
Belvoir	Beever
Hawick	Hoik
Holyhead	Holly-head
Lympne	Lim
Marylebone	Marry-le-bon
Mousehole	Mowzel
Oswaldtwistle	Ozzel-twizzle
Ravenstruther	Renstree
Rievaulx	Reevo
Welwyn	Wellin
Udny	Widnee

NATTY NAMES AND TITLES

The naming of people, places and things has led to some of the finest and strangest wordplay in English. Many names are ordinary, of course, but many are amusing, strange, puzzling or plain nutty. The people who came up with the names in this section certainly had their imaginations cranked up that day...

What the Dickens?

The great English author Charles Dickens (not Darles Chickens as the Rev Spooner might have known him*) wrote sixteen of the most popular novels of any age. He was a master of our language who created an astounding cast of fantastical characters in his stories, with names such as Fezziwig, Honeythunder and Noddy Boffin. Here are some more of his minor players and the books in which they appeared.

Serjeant Buzfuz Pickwick Papers
Anne Chickenstalker **The Chimes**
General Fladdock Martin Chuzzlewit
Newman Noggs **Nicholas Nickleby**

Mercy Pecksniff Martin Chuzzlewit
Phil Squod **Bleak House**
Milly Swidger The Haunted Man
Nathaniel Winkle **Pickwick Papers**

* See page 68.

Shakespearean Shtyle

William Shakespeare's plays are still performed around the world every day, nearly 400 years after his death. He created hundreds of diverse characters including a group with curious names...

Character	Play
Sir Toby Belch	Twelfth Night
Bottom	A Midsummer Night's Dream
Dull	Love's Labours Lost
Elbow	Measure for Measure
Feeble	Henry IV, Part 2
Old Gobbo	The Merchant of Venice
Hugh Oatcake	Much Ado About Nothing
Pistol	The Merry Wives of Windsor
Rynaldo	All's Well That Ends Well
Wart	Henry IV, Part 2

Just Nutty Names

Here is a fruity assortment of amusing and curious people from books, films, TV, radio, theatre, music and comedy:

Po Nudo
An alarmingly-toothed alien from the Stars Wars films

Dr Hugo Z. Hackenbush
A character played by Groucho Marx in the film A Day at the Races

Cletus Spuckler
The 'slack-jawed yokel' from the TV animation The Simpsons

Alexander Throttlebottom
From the musical Let 'Em Eat Cake (lyrics by Ira Gershwin)

Grima Wormtongue
An unpleasant individual featured in the Lord of the Rings novels by JRR Tolkien

Nigel Incubator-Jones
An upper-class twit from Monty Python's Flying Circus

Everett Kroopenhooper
Character from an early Mickey Mouse comic

Augustus Fink-Nottle
A recurring individual in PG Wodehouse's Jeeves stories.

Ood
A monster/alien from Doctor Who

Zaphod Beeblebrox
A two-headed chap from The Hitchiker's Guide to the Galaxy chronicles by Douglas Adams

Interesting American Towns

Amazingly, these are all real names. Whoever chose them had LOTS of imagination...

Boring	(Oregon)
Accident	(Maryland)
Monkey's Eyebrow	(Kentucky)
Jollytown	(Pennsylvania)
King of Prussia	(Pennsylvania)
Normal	(Illinois)
Peculiar	(Missouri)
Secret Town	(California)
Tacky Town	(Kentucky)
The Y	(West Virginia)
Tiny Town	(Colorado)
Wahoo	(Florida)
Cheesequake	(New Jersey)

Rather Rude UK Place Names

These speak for themselves:

Backside – Aberdeenshire
Scratchy Bottom – Dorset
Trump Street – London
Panty Hill – Powys
North Piddle – Worcestershire

Butt of Lewis – Outer Hebrides
Fartown – West Yorkshire
Pratt's Bottom – Kent
Buttock – Lancashire
Brokenwind – Aberdeenshire

I was born on Muck...

Here is a list of intriguing Scottish Islands:

- Bigga
- Yell
- Muckle Flugga
- Rum
- Papa Little
- Rough
- Wart Holm
- Muck

Wacky Inns

Forget The Kings Arms or the Coach and Horses – here are some pubs with pzazz:

The Goat and Tricycle – Bournemouth

The Mad Moose – Norwich

The Barmy Arms – Twickenham

The Bucket of Blood – Phillack

Nobody Inn – Dartmoor

The World's End – Patching

The Muscular Arms – Glasgow

Howl at the Moon – Dublin

The One-Eyed Rat – Ripon

The Rorty Crankle – Plaxtol

My Father's Moustache – Louth

Q – Stalybridge

They call me The -

Some people are so well known that their names enter into legend and they become known as 'The something'. You'll know some of these but perhaps not all:

The Face that launched a thousand ships (Mythical Helen of Troy, whose abduction by the Trojans led the Greeks to send a vast invasion fleet)

The Maid of Orléans (Joan of Arc, the French teenage warrior and visionary burnt at the stake by the English in 1431)

The Little Corporal (Napoleon Bonaparte, the small military leader who conquered big countries)

The Lady with the Lamp (Florence Nightingale, who nursed soldiers injured in the Crimean War)

The Duke (John Wayne, big, slow-talkin' cowboy actor)

The King of Rock 'n' Roll (Elvis Presley, hip-swivelling, mega-selling early pop icon)

The Beast of Bolsover (Dennis Skinner, shouty left-wing Labour MP and ex-miner)

The Great Gonzo (purple daredevil Muppet)

The Bald Eagle (Jim Smith, hairless old-school manager of ten different football clubs)

The Queen of Soul (Aretha Franklin, U.S. singer with 88 hits)

The Hoff (David Hasselhoff, cult hairy-chested star of Baywatch TV series in the 1990s)

The Refrigerator (William Perry, 150kg kitchen appliance-like American footballer)

The Great White Shark (Greg Norman, tall blond Aussie golfing champ)

The Power (Phil Taylor, undisputed world darts number one, from Stoke)

The Non-Flying Dutchman (Denis Bergkamp, ex-Arsenal striker fearful of air travel)

Nicknames of note: sporty people

Sports fans love a good nickname and here are some choice ones from the worlds of bats, balls and bikes:

Nickname	Person	Sporting achievement
Pretty Boy	Floyd Mayweather Jr	Undefeated American boxer who managed to avoid the usual scars and bent nose
Stella the Fella	Stella Walsh	A Polish athlete who won Olympic gold. Tests after her death showed that she may have been male.
The Thorpedo	Ian Thorpe	Six foot five Aussie who won loads of medals at the 2000 Olympics. Loads.
Two-metre Peter	Peter Fulton	A cricketer, this towering New Zealand batsman stands nearly six feet seven, which is 2m.

Nickname	Person	Sporting achievement
The Incredible Sulk	Nicolas Anelka	French footballer, recently of West Brom, renowned for looking miserable.
Swiss Miss	Martina Hingis	Tennis champ from Switzerland who won five Grand Slam titles.
Chariots	Martin Offiah	Lightning quick British rugby player, nicknamed after the film Chariots of Fire.
Whispering Death	Michael Holding	Tall, quiet and savagely fast-bowling cricketer from the great 1970s West Indies team.
One Size	Fitz Hall	English footballer whose nickname is based on the old advertising claim, 'One size fits all'.
Boom-Boom	Boris Becker	German tennis player who won Wimbledon when just 17 – his big booming serve led to the title.
Bonecrusher	James Smith	American heavyweight boxer with a ferocious punch.

A varied collection of individuals

Do you know what a grockle is, or a jobsworth? This mini-glossary of people will hopefully reduce your ignorance:

TOFF a very posh individual.

YOKEL a country bumpkin.

COUCH POTATO someone who watches too much TV.

GOTH a follower of dark music and clothes.

WHITE VAN MAN unruly male delivery driver.

GROCKLE a tourist.

OIK a lout.

HOORAY HENRY a noisy male toff.

LADETTE a boisterous young woman.

TOWNIE a city dweller who knows little about the country.

CODGER a grumpy old man.

JOBSWORTH an employee who does everything by the rules, avoiding common sense.

SPROG a baby or small kid.

NIMBY a person who protests against building developments near his or her home (abbreviation of 'Not in my back yard').

Footballers allowed in Scrabble

Proper names are not allowed in the word game Scrabble, but if the names are also ordinary words they are:

Hart – 7pts

Noble – 7pts

Bent – 6pts

Brown – 10pts

Sterling – 9pts

Young – 9pts

Duff – 11pts

Baker – 11pts

Parker – 12pts

Marshall – 13pts

Walker – 13pts

Fletcher – 16pts

Regional nicknames

People in Britain like to give each other nicknames, for some reason, and some of them are pleasingly playful. Enjoy this brief guide to some of the daft titles we call each other.

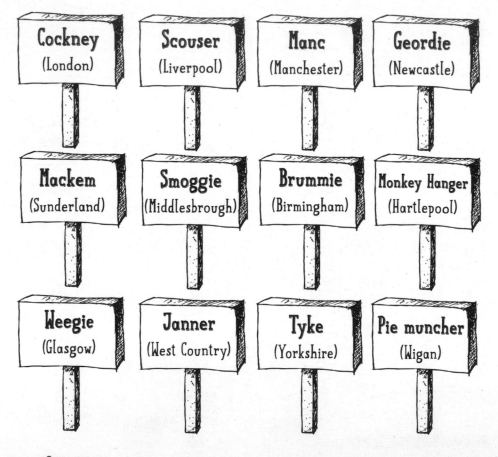

Cockney (London)

Scouser (Liverpool)

Manc (Manchester)

Geordie (Newcastle)

Mackem (Sunderland)

Smoggie (Middlesbrough)

Brummie (Birmingham)

Monkey Hanger (Hartlepool)

Weegie (Glasgow)

Janner (West Country)

Tyke (Yorkshire)

Pie muncher (Wigan)

Strange song titles

Lots of song titles are strange and some are funny but these ones also whoop up the wordplay:

Bish Bash Bosh Jook, 1974

Hubba Hubba Zoot Zoot Caramba, 1981

Bang Bang Bang Mark Ronson, 2010

Ob La Di Ob La Da The Beatles, 1968

Rama Lama Ding Dong The Edsels, 1961

Itsy Bitsy Teeny Weeny Yellow Polka Dot Bikini Brian Hyland, 1960

Too Pooped to Pop Chuck Berry, 1960

Skooby Oobly Doobob Ten Years After, 1969

Place aliases

Some of these are a bit silly. Quiz your friends or family and see how many they know:

The Big Smoke – **London**

The Pond – **Atlantic Ocean**

The Big Apple – **New York**

The Eternal City – **Rome**

Brum – **Birmingham**

The Emerald Isle – **Ireland**

The Granite City – **Aberdeen**

The Sunshine State – **Florida**

Auld Reekie – **Edinburgh**

Blighty – **Great Britain**

The Windy City – **Chicago**

Oz – **Australia**

The Garden of England – **Kent**

The Land of the Rising Sun – **Japan**

The Big Easy – **New Orleans**

The City of Dreaming Spires – **Oxford**

The Queen of the Adriatic – **Venice**

Land of a Thousand Lakes – **Finland**

The City of Love – **Paris**

God's Own County – **Yorkshire**

Nicknames for everything

It's not just people that have nicknames. Places, vehicles and all sorts of things have alternative titles, some of which are affectionate and some silly.

The Flying Cow – the slow, lumbering Avro Shackleton warplane

Hairy Ass – cheeky title for warship USS Harry S. Truman

Frankenstorm – Hurricane Sandy, a giant storm that crossed America in 2012

Auntie – The BBC which, in its early days, was thought of as a bit bossy and dull.

The Tin Lizzie – The Model T Ford, an early popular car

Marks and Sparks – Cherished chain store Marks and Spencers, famed for selling tons of knickers

Penny Farthing – the early, giant-wheeled 'Ordinary bicycle'

The Gherkin – vegetable-like high-rise office building in London

Spaghetti Junction – a famous motorway interchange near Birmingham where several roads meet

Gronk – the British Rail Class 08 diesel locomotive, a common dull engine

The Old Lady – famous Italian football club Juventus, one of the first in the country.

SPIFFING SPOONERISMS

The Reverend Spooner was a legendary church minister and Oxford University don (even though his name was William Archibald, not Don) who was around about 100 years ago. Spooner became famous for 'wixing up his murds' in a special way, often accidentally swapping the sounds at the beginning of words in a sentence. These slips of the tongue are now called Spoonerisms.

The Rev Spooner is remembered at New College, Oxford where the Middle Common Room is affectionately known as 'The Rooner Spoom'.

Spoken by Spooner?

It's claimed that The Rev Spooner spoke these classic spoonerisms himself, mostly while lecturing students at Oxford University. Perhaps he didn't actually say them all, but it's chucklesome fun to imagine it happening...

'You hissed my mystery lecture.' (You missed my history lecture)

'Is the bean dizzy?' (Is the dean busy?)

'You have tasted two worms.'
(You have wasted two terms)

'A well-boiled icicle' (A well-oiled bicycle)

'He was killed by a blushing crow.'
(He was killed by a crushing blow)

'Three cheers for our queer old dean!'
(Three cheers for our dear old queen)

Church shockers

The Rev Spooner, being a priest as well as an academic, often gave sermons in church. Here are some of the things he is supposed to have said:

'It is kisstomary to cuss the bride.' (It is customary to kiss the bride)

'The Lord is a shoving leopard.' (The Lord is a loving shepherd)

'I see before me tons of soil.' (I see before me sons of toil)

'... a half-warmed fish' (A half-formed wish)

'This pie is occupewed. Can I sew you to another sheet?' (This pew is occupied. Can I show you to another seat?)

Quoonerism Spiz

See if you can work out these spoonerisms. For example 'bowel feast' = foul beast. The answers are on page 156.

☞ Belly jeans
☞ Mad banners
☞ Bat flattery
☞ I shook a tower
☞ Lack of pies

☞ Bunny phone
☞ Sealing the hick
☞ Door of fireman's
☞ Fighting a liar
☞ Fart smeller

More tips of the slung

Many of us have accidentally said 'par cark' but just occasionally people come out with spoonerisms which are unintentionally comical, such as these:

'It's roaring with pain outside, dear.' (It's pouring with rain outside, dear)

'We'll have the hags flung out for the party.' (We'll have the flags hung out for the party)

'Put that soul of ballad on the table.' (Put that bowl of salad on the table)

'Stop nicking your pose, Charles.' (Stop picking your nose, Charles)

'I wouldn't like to live in that flock of bats.' (I wouldn't like to live in that block of flats)

'Sprinkle on some chopped nasal huts.' (Sprinkle on some chopped hazelnuts)

'Granny's taken the last sparking pace.' (Granny's taken the last parking space)

'Oh, he's always trying to wave the sails.' (Oh, he's always trying to save the whales)

70

Mangled media

Here are some spoonerised books, films, TV shows and more for your enjoyment — the spellings are changed so that they are easier to read and say aloud.

- ✪ <u>Pinnie the Wooh</u> (book) — <u>Winnie the Pooh</u>
- ✪ <u>Bleeping Seauty</u> (fairy tale) — <u>Sleeping Beauty</u>
- ✪ <u>Dooby Scoo</u> (TV show) — <u>Scooby Doo</u>
- ✪ <u>Some Hike it Lot</u> (film) — <u>Some Like it Hot</u>
- ✪ <u>Bet it Lee</u> (song) — <u>Let it Be</u>
- ✪ <u>Breadknobs and Boomsticks</u> (film) — <u>Bedknobs ad Broomsticks</u>
- ✪ <u>The Hat in the Cat</u> (book) — <u>The Cat in the Hat</u>
- ✪ <u>Bus in Poots</u> (fairy tale) — <u>Puss in Boots</u>
- ✪ <u>The Shaming of the True</u> (play) — <u>The Taming of the Shrew</u>
- ✪ <u>Poo Bleater</u> (TV show) — <u>Blue Peter</u>
- ✪ <u>Baddington Pear</u> (book) — <u>Paddington Bear</u>
- ✪ <u>Dawn of the Shed</u> (film) — <u>Shaun of the Dead</u>
- ✪ <u>God Rest Ye Gerry Mentlemen</u> (song) — <u>God Rest Ye Merry Gentlemen</u>
- ✪ <u>Ringing in the Sane</u> (song) — <u>Singing in the Rain</u>
- ✪ <u>To Thatch a Keith</u> (film) — <u>To Catch a Thief</u>

WITTY WORDPLAY POEMS

Some of the choicest wordplay is to be found in poems and, indeed, poets have been tickling readers' fancies with wordy wit for thousands of years. Here is verse, odes, rhymes, non-rhymes, limericks, doggerel and catterel*.

*This word is possibly made up

Yak in the Attic

I was searching in the attic
When I found a dusty yak it
Raced around the back it
Was scared and made a racket.
It hid, I couldn't track it,
It must have thought I'd whack it
Or simply try to stack it,
Or find a box and pack it.

Its fear was automatic,
When I found it, it stood static,
So I had a chance to vac it,
Which might seem a bit drastic.
But I never did attack it,
Or push or pull or smack it,
For I was really quite ecstatic –
To find a yak up in the attic!

Coral Rumble

Parent Problem Solved

Mum and Dad demand respect,
They say that they're my betters.
But I can make them Dum and Mad
By changing round two letters.

Jasper Bark

Bury My Heart at Wounded Knee

Bury my heart at Wounded Knee,
Bury my liver on the M63.

Bury my lungs in Ross-on-Wye,
Bury my bottom with a slice of pie.

Bury my spleen at the top of a hill,
Bury my guts on the window sill.

Bury my eyes in a bucket of glue,
Bury my kidneys at a quarter past two.

Bury my brain in next door's shed,
But do me a favour and wait till I'm dead.

Andy Seed

The Boys in My Class

The boys
In my class
Can't keep
Still:
Bob'll bobble
Jack'll cackle
Rob'll wobble
Tom'll tackle
Tod'll toddle
Sid'll fiddle
Wilf'll waddle
Tim'll twiddle
Mat'll battle
Nick'll tickle
Pat'll rattle
Pete'll prickle
Rab'll babble
Stig'll wiggle
Guy'll gabble
And Jef'll jiggle.
See.

Andy Seed

HA

HA

HA!

Limericks

Limericks are one of the most popular ways to wordplay.
These five-line funnies are good fun to learn off by heart.

The sea-cow or grey manatee
Spends most of its time in the sea,
But in tropical rainstorms
It suffers from brainstorms
And hangs upside down in a tree.

Anonymous

An elderly fellow named Keith,
Mislaid his set of false teeth.
He was quite unaware,
They were left on a chair;
He sat down – and was bitten beneath.

Anonymous

A canner exceedingly canny,
One morning remarked to his granny,
'A canner can can
Anything that he can,
But a canner can't can a can, can he?'

Carolyn Wells

75

I sat next to the duchess at tea,
It was just as I feared it would be;
Her rumblings abdominal
Were simply phenomenal
And everyone thought it was me.

Anonymous

There once was a young chef of Crewe
Who was hired despite lacking a clue;
Whilst adding shallot,
He fell in the pot,
But he did make an excellent stew.

Andy Seed

There was a young fellow named Fisher,
Who was fishing for fish in a fissure,
When a cod with a grin
Pulled the fisherman in...
Now they're fishing the fissure for Fisher.

Anonymous

A traveller once to his sorrow,
Requested a ticket to Morrow.
Said the railman, 'It's plain
That there isn't a train
To Morrow today, but tomorrow.'

Anonymous

Lampooning limericks

Some limericks make fun of the peculiar spellings of certain names and places.
Can you work out these playful poems?

There was an old man of Nantucket
Who kept all his cash in a bucket;
But his daughter, named Nan,
Ran away with a man,
And as for the bucket, Nantucket.

Anonymous

The incredible Wizard of Oz
Retired from his business becoz
Due to uptodate science,
To most of his clients,
He wasn't the wiz that he woz.

Anonymous

There was a young girl in the choir
Whose voice rose hoir and hoir;
Till it reached such a height
It was clear out of seight,
And they found it next day on the spoir.

Anonymous

A lively young damsel named Menzies*
Enquired, 'Do you know what this thenzies?'
    Her aunt, with a gasp,
    Replied, 'It's a wasp,
And you're holding the end where the stenzies.'

Anonymous

[*The name Menzies is pronounced 'ming-iss']

There was a young lady of Twickenham,
Whose boots were too tight to walk quickenham.
    She bore them awhile,
    But at last, at a stile,
She pulled them both off and was sickenham.

Anonymous

Punny Poems

Few are the poets who dabble not in pun fun from time to time.
Just sit back and enjoy these...

Yeti

He's in the Himalayas, yeti
    hasn't been found,
He leaves us great big footprints, yeti
    doesn't make a sound.
He doesn't live on garlic bread
    or meatballs, or spaghetti –
There's nothing there to eat, yeti
    does, yeti does.

He is a sort of snowman, yeti
    won't melt in the sun,
A kind of 'I don't know' man, yeti's
    definitely one
Or maybe only half a man,
    don't know, we haven't met, he
isn't really real yeti
is, yeti is.

He's never been measured, yeti's
    seven metres tall,
He lives in snowy places, yeti
    can't get cold at all,
His abominable woman
    is the kind you can't forget, he
Could be getting married yeti
    won't, yeti won't.

Ros Barber

Pelican Curry

A pelican curry
is a hot and spicy thrill,
the only real problem -
the whacking great bill!

Matt Goodfellow

On the Very First Valentine's Day

What the caveman gave his missus—
lots and lots of ughs and kisses.

Graham Denton

Puzzling poems

Some poems are mysteries in verse which need to be solved. Can you puzzle out this one?

School Trip Quotes

(A poem for a class having a day out at the seaside)

'Are we nearly there yet?' said Miles.
'Aw, it's taking ages,' said Mona.
'I don't feel well,' said Chuck.
'Oh, you'll be fine,' said Faith.
'Let's have a sing-song,' said Carol.
'The sun's out at last,' said Ray.
'What a wonderful day,' said Joy.
'Let's go to the beach,' said Sandy.
'Yeah - and build sandcastles,' said Doug.
'I want to fish in rock pools,' said Annette.
'Don't go near the edge,' said Cliff.
'And mind the stones,' said Rocky.
'Are there any wild animals round here?' said Claude.
'I need a drink,' said Phil.
'Make mine a big one,' said Max.
'How much do they cost?' said Bill.
'This one was free,' said Nick.
'Can we go now? I need a wee,' said Lou.

Andy Seed

Odd odes

Miscellaneous moments from the pens of people who let words run willy-nilly through their imaginations.

On Tuesdays I Polish My Uncle

I went to play in the park.
I didn't get home until dark.
But when I got back I had ants in my pants
And my father was feeding the shark.

I went to play in the park.
And I didn't come home until dark.
And when I got back I had ants in my pants
Dirt in my shirt, glue in my shoe,
And my father was tickling the shark.

I went to sleep in the park.
The shark was starting to bark.
And when I woke up I had ants in my pants,
Dirt in my shirt, glue in my shoe,
And beans in my jeans and a bee on my knee,
And the shark was tickling my father.

My father went off to the park.
I stayed home and read to the shark.
And when he got back he had ants in his pants,
Dirt in his shirt, glue in his shoe,
Beans in his jeans, a bee on his knee,
Beer in his ear and a bear in his hair,
So we put him outside in the ark.

I started the ark in the dark.
My father was parking the shark.
And when we got home we had ants in our pants,
Dirt in our shirt, glue in our shoe,
Beans in our jeans, a bee on our knee,
Beer in our ear and a bear in our hair,
A stinger on each finger, a stain in our brain,
And our belly-buttons shone in the dark.

So my dad he got snarky and barked at the shark.
Who was parking the ark on the mark in the dark.
And when they got back they had ants in their pants,
Dirt in their shirt, glue in their shoe,
Beans in their jeans, a bee on their knee,
Beer in their ear and a bear in their hair,
A stinger in each finger, a stain in their brain,
A small polka-dot burp, with headache tablets,
And a ship on the lip and a horse, of course,
So we all took a bath in the same tub and went to bed early.

Dennis Lee

Spelling Test

The worst thing
to get
in a spelling test
is diarrhoea.

Andy Seed

Some unusual weather conditions

If smoke + fog = smog, then...

frost + fog = frog

snow + hail = snail

mist + ice = mice

chilly + damp = champ

fog + drizzle = frizzle

wind + blizzards = wizards

chilly + breezy = cheesy

crisp + gusty = crusty

condensation + stillness + precipitation = constipation

Mike Barfield

The Rev Spooner's Favourite Olympic Events

Vole pault
Leightwifting
Pot Shutt
Ji skumping
Madbinton
Pater wolo
Veach bolleyball
Bountain miking
Tenpathlon
Jigh hump
Jong lump
Jiple trump
Skigure fating
Weestyle frestling
And
Table Tennis
(Hank Theavens)

Andy Seed

EPITAPHS

Epitaphs are messages written about someone who has died. Often poetic, they are found on gravestones and most of them are serious and worthy but just occasionally they delight. Here is a mixture of real ones and funny fakes.

These epitaphs are from real gravestones:

Here lays Butch.
We planted him raw.
He was quick on the trigger
But slow on the draw.
(Boot Hill Cemetery,
Tombstone, Arizona)

Stranger tread
This ground with gravity.
Dentist Brown
Is filling his last cavity.
(Edinburgh, Scotland)

Here lies Dr Keene,
the good Bishop of
Chester,
Who ate up a fat
goose, but could not
digest her.
(Cheshire)

This tombstone is a
Milestone;
Hah! How so?
Because beneath
lies Miles, who's
Miles below.
(Cumbria)

Beneath this smooth stone
By the bone of his bone,
Sleeps Master John Gill;
By lies when alive this
attorney did thrive,
And now that he's dead
he lies still.
(unknown location)

Here lies the
body of W.W.
Who never more
will trouble you,
trouble you.
(London: the grave of
William Wilson)

Owen Moore
Gone away
Owin' more
Than he could pay.
(Battersea, London)

He passed the bobby
without any fuss,
And he passed the cart
of hay.
He tried to pass a
swerving bus,
And then he passed away.
(unknown location)

Here lies one Wood
Enclosed in wood
One Wood
Within another.
The outer wood
Is very good;
We cannot praise
The other.
(Winslow, USA: the grave of Beza Wood)

Here lies one
Blown out of breath
Who lived a merry life
And died a Merideth.
(Oxford: the grave of Mr
Merideth)

A SLICE O' SLANG

Have you ever been told off for using slang? We all do it – we use words that aren't quite the 'proper' ones but convey what we want to say in a casual way. Sometimes slang can upset people who want us to speak correctly but it is also a creative form of wordplay which can be fun to use for people who have the same interests. Just be careful with it near parents, teachers, and er... Her Majesty....

How's your vernacular?

Vernacular language refers to everyday words and expressions, some of which may be regarded as a bit informal or slightly rude, depending on the company – so be careful who you say them to!

nipper
whipper-snapper
kiddie
scamp
Child
brat
tyke
bairn
ankle biter
tot

Food

scoff
grub
snap
tucker
nosh
eats
chow
tuck
scran
vittles

Money

dosh
bread
dough
mazuma
wonga
moolah
loot
readies
spondulicks
lolly

Toilet

loo
thunderbox
khazi
lavvy
can
bog
po
dunny
throne
john

Mouth

trap
gob
kisser
mush
yap
cakehole
piehole
maw
chops

Nose

schnozzle
whiffer
conk
honker
snout
beak
hooter
snotlocker

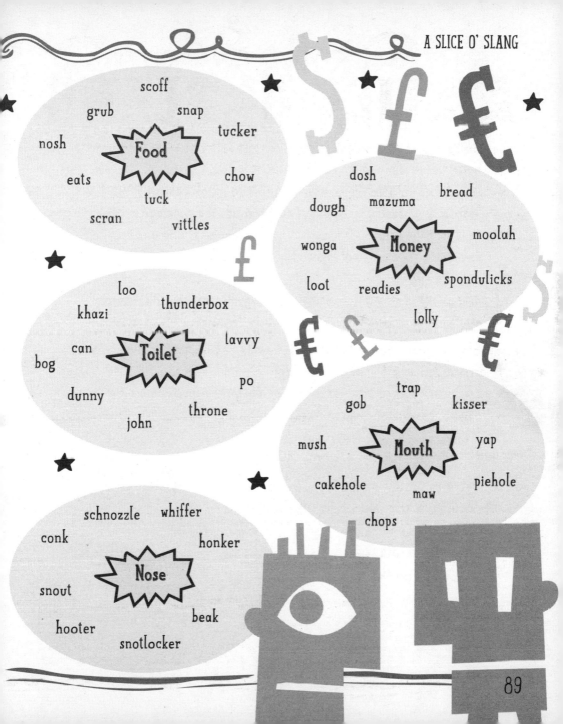

89

Jocular terms

English is full of jokey phrases which are not proper words or expressions (as found in most dictionaries) but are widely used between people having light-hearted conversations.

Absitively posolutely – spoonerised blend of absolutely and positively, meaning certainly

Any fule kno – 'any fool knows': the catchphrase of fictional schoolboy Nigel Molesworth

Ba-dum ching – imitation of a drum roll and cymbal crash used to acknowledge a gag

Dihydrogen monoxide – humorous term for water, used to catch people out

Discombobulate – to befuddle someone

Edumacate – deliberate misspelling of educate for comic effect

Extract the Michael – take the mickey

Frankenfood – genetically modified eats

Gruntle – the opposite of disgruntle

Living impaired – dead

Make like a tree and leave – to depart

Me three – added onto 'me too' as a form of agreement

Round tuit – a mythical circular object enabling a person to get things done (a play on 'I'll do that when I get around to it.')

Smell ya later – silly alternative to 'see you later'

Squillionaire – a mega-rich person

Cockney rhyming slang

Cockney rhyming slang is a form of wordplay that developed a long time ago in the East End of London. It uses rhyming substitutes for words (often abbreviating them, just to confuse everyone). Here are some common examples:

Word	Short for	Meaning
apples	apples and pears	stairs
jam	jam jar	car
dog	dog and bone	phone
plates	plates of meat	feet
raspberry	raspberry tart	fart
boat	boat race	face
mince	mince pie	eye
loaf	loaf of bread	head
china	china plate	mate
whistle	whistle and flute	suit
frog	frog and toad	road
bread	bread and honey	money

How it works

If you wanted to tell someone to park their car on the road, for example, you would say 'Park your jam on the frog.'

91

Hi spec colloquialisms

Colloquialisms is a posh word for slang – these are everyday words and expressions that people use in place of standard words because they are fun, cheeky or just add variety to the lingo.

attagirl	used to show encouragement to a young female
booyah	an exclamation of satisfaction or excitement
gut buster	a very large meal
keep schtum	don't tell anyone
lovely jubbly	marvellous
mozzie	a mosquito
nada	nothing (from the Spanish word)
natch	naturally
nitty gritty	the core of something
phizog	face
shark bait	a lone swimmer at sea
sling yer hook	leave
snot rag	hanky
spec	specification: the features of something
throw a wobbly	lose your temper
weepie	a sad or romantic film
wind-up merchant	a joker

Baby talk

Can you think of any more?

beddy-byes

choo-choo

bow-wow

botty

gee-gee

hurty

itty bitty

ickle

meeces

moo-moo

num-num

whoopsie

yucky

teeny weeny

tinkle

scaredy cat

Street speak

'Slanguage' is changing and developing all of the time, especially the words used by young people in big cities like London. Expressions quickly go out of fashion, however, so these phrases may soon be, well, pants...

Street word	Meaning
Baggamanz	Lots
Ginchy	Cool
Garms	Clothes
Hench	Muscular
Kotch	To chill out
Zories	Flip flops
Nang	Good
reh teh teh	etc.
Skadoosh	Goodbye
Skeen	I see
Wagwan	What's going on?

Internet slang

As the web has grown so has its own language and wordplay. A lot of internet slang is abbreviation to make typing quicker but some has developed from the technology itself and some from new features of social media sites or viral internet humour events.

n00b
new user

G2G
got to go

teh
deliberate typo
meaning the

FOMO
fear of missing out –
the worry that all the
action is taking place
somewhere else

IMO
In my
opinion

troll
a person who
deliberately stirs
up trouble on
the web

selfie
photo you take
of yourself

unfriend
to remove a friend
from Facebook or
a similar site

nom nom nom
refers to
something
yummy

tl;dr
too long; didn't
read – referring to
a long, boring post

derp
refers to somethig
silly or stupid

Football lingo

Players, managers, commentators, pundits and footy fans spend a lot of time speaking in a peculiar kind of code. This will help you unravel their gibberish:

Expression	Meaning
Bang out of order	Wrong
Big ask	Difficult task
Big unit	Hefty player
Bottle	Courage
Chasing shadows	When a team cannot get the ball
Different class	Excellent
Dig	Shot
Early doors	The first part of a game
Fox in the box	Proven goal poacher

Expression	Meaning
Hairdryer treatment	Being shouted at by a grumpy manager
Left peg	Left foot
Mare	Short for 'nightmare'
Mind games	Something crafty said to unsettle an opponent
Mixer	Where lots of players are in the penalty box
Take positives	Clutch at straws
The red mist	When a player loses all control of his temper
Top drawer	Very good
To be fair	(Has no meaning)

Biker dictionary

Motorcycle enthusiasts, like all subcultures, have their very own words and phrases for things which are familiar to them. Here are some of the best:

Ape hangers
high handlebars

Belly shover
a motorbike racer

Giggle gas
nitrous oxide, used to give a power boost

Monkey butt
a sore botty, from too much riding

Twisties
part of a road with lots of tight bends

Stinkwheel
a noisy two-stroke bike

Swapping paint
when two riders in a group accidentally bump machines

Yard shark
a bike-bothering dog

Brain bucket
Helmet

Surfer cipher

Here is some patter beloved of those dudes who spend all day hanging around on the beach and riding big waves.

Ankle snapper
tiny wave

Beef
a problem with someone

Brosiah
a surfer's hero

Dudette
female surfer friend

Goat boater
kayaker who gets in the way

Perf
Awesome

Rad
Great, cool

Vacay
Holiday

Flushopolis
when waves are too close together

Woot
Cool

99

OTHER PEOPLE'S ENGLISH

English is the official language of quite a few countries around the world but every one of these places will have its own unique set of words and therefore its own wordplay. Even different regions of countries have their own slang, expressions, pronunciation and meanings. This is why the word 'eh?' is so popular...

Regional parlance

People in different parts of Britain sometimes use different words for different things. This was more common in the past. Here's a wee sample:

Mum
ma (Belfast), mam (Liverpool), mom (Birmingham)

Hello
how do (York), wotcha (London), now then (Sheffield), alreet (Newcastle)

Plimsolls
daps (Plymouth), sand shoes (Scotland), pumps (Dartford), gutties (N. Ireland)

Trousers
breeks (Edinburgh), kecks (Wigan), duds (Glasgow)

Attractive
tidy (Cardiff), fit (Manchester), buff (London), gert lush (Bristol)

Friendly terms of address

People in different parts of the world call strangers all sorts of things when they don't know their name...

Boss	Duck	Mate
Boyo	Fella	Missus
Bro	Guv	Pal
Buddy	Honey	Pet
Chief	Love	Sister
Chum	Mac	Son
Cobber		Sport
Darling		Sugar
Dearie		Sunshine
Dude		Sweetheart

Oz and them

Australians have some great laid-back expressions for all sorts of things – here's a little selection:

Oldies parents

Milko milkman

Yewy a u-turn

Bodgy of low quality

Shark biscuit novice surfer

Bush telly a camp fire

Ripper great/brilliant

Ute pickup truck (utility vehicle)

Sunnies sunglasses

Pozzy position, as in a good place to sit

Dunny outside loo

Ankle biter young child

Our mates in the States

Here are some Americanisms that have appeared over the years:

Some words Americans use that Brits don't
Airplane (aeroplane)
Ballpark (baseball stadium)
Booger (bogey)
Critter (creature)
Faucet (tap)
Pantyhose (tights)

American pronunciation

Word	How they say it in the US
coupe	'coop'
herbs	'urbs'
lever	'levver'
premiere	'premeer'
Van Gogh	'Van Go'
Route	'rowt'
Vase	'vace'
yoghurt	'yowgurt'
Z	'zee'

US Slang

Boo-boo	mistake
Far-out	Great
Flip out	go berserk
Goof up	get something badly wrong
Honcho	Boss
Jock	athlete
Mellow out	Relax
Rack out	Sleep
Slammer	Prison
Zip	nothing

Coined in the States

A lot of English expressions that people use today come from the USA originally. Do you know these?

Phrase	Meaning
The bee's knees	Fantastic
A blast from the past	things or people that return after absence
A dead ringer	an exact lookalike
Fancy pants	a showy person
Gung ho	over eager
The heebie-jeebies	severe doubt and worry
Hunky-dory	all good
Know your onions	to know a lot about something
On cloud nine	blissfully happy
Pie in the sky	something hoped for
Smoke and mirrors	Trickery
Spill the beans	to tell a secret
Top notch	Excellent

Global gobbledygook

Here are bits of English spoken around the world that might confuse foreign visitors:

Acting pricey
In India this means 'playing hard to get' or not making time for your friends.

Pass me the chilly bin
A chilly bin in New Zealand is a cool box.

Chop-chop
This means 'hurry up' and came from English sailors copying a Cantonese word in China meaning 'be quick'.

Had the biscuit
From Canada: this means broken or dead.

Kill the TV
Not a call to violence but simply a request to switch off the telly in the Philippines

What's your proggie?
In Uganda this means 'what are your social plans?'

Long time no see
A phrase based on broken English spoken by an American Indian, and now widely used in the UK.

Well past it: ancestral wordplay

Wordplay is as old as language itself. Here is a bit of antique wit:

In Ancient Greece, the great philosopher Socrates is supposed to have devised the clever saying,

'Eat to live, not live to eat.'

William Shakespeare loved to pen a pun and his plays are full of them. For example, in Romeo and Juliet, the character Mercutio is fatally stabbed and with his dying breath says,

'Ask for me to-morrow, and you shall find me a grave man.'

Grave meaning serious and a place for bodies, of course

Blockbuster Victorian novelist Charles Dickens incorporated wordplay into his books through names. One example is Nicholas Nickleby which features a lad-bashing school called Dotheboys Hall run by a brute called Wackford Squeers.

Edward Lear, famous writer of Limericks and nonsense verse enjoyed making up new words without meanings, one of the most famous being his 'runcible spoon' from the poem, The Owl and the Pussycat.

A recurring gag in music halls of the early 20th century featured a bow-legged butler who answers the door and says,

'Walk this way'.

The person invited in then copies his comic waddle.

Those certainly are chaic

Archaic words are old 'uns that are hardly ever used any more, except maybe to raise a giggle. But actually some of these phrases are rather enjoyable...

daffadowndilly
Daffodil

huzzah
Hooray

griggling
collecting small apples

flabbergastation
bewildered shock

pittle-pattle
Chatter

nudle
to walk quickly with
head bent forward

tiggy-touchwood
a children's game like tag

knut
an idle rich chap

yield up the ghost
to die

zyxt
means 'seen' in Old English

By the way, 'zyxt' is the last word of
about **300,000** in the full Oxford English
Dictionary.

MISCELLANEOUS MALARKEY

This section is a random celebration of verbal verve and all sorts of curious word twiddling. For many of the lists you can have a go at adding your own examples.

Puntastic banners

Some newspapers can't print a headline without a wayward pun but just occasionally they come up with something smart and amusing, like these.

ANDRE VILLAS GOAS!

The paper's way of suggesting that football team Spurs should sack their manager Andre Villas Boas.

Daily Mirror

CELEBRITY BIG BLUBBER

Headline for a picture of a whale which accidentally swam up the river Thames and got stuck in London.

The Sun

YO HO D'OH!

A report about the crew of a ship foiling an attack by modern pirates off the African coast.

New York Post

KATE EXPECTATIONS!

To announce that the Duchess of Cambridge, Kate Middleton, was pregnant.

The Sun

A WAYNE IN A MANGER

A story about a couple naming their new baby after footballer Wayne Rooney.

Liverpool Echo

RAINE, RAINE GO AWAY

Heading of a bad review of a Craig Raine poetry book.

The Observer

109

Proverbial pandemonium

These well-known sayings are just a tad mixed up — see if you can sort out the right endings. Answers on page 157.

- A bird in the hand is worth two in the cat.
- Blood is thicker than boys.
- Boys will be right.
- Curiosity killed the bush.
- Don't put all your eggs in one broth.
- In for a penny, in for a tango.
- It's no use crying over spilt one.
- It takes two to leap.
- Look before you cure.
- Never look a gift horse in the basket.
- Prevention is better than milk.
- Too many cooks spoil the mouth.
- Two heads are better than ears
- Two wrongs do not make a pound.
- Walls have water.

Portmanteau creations

One of the things that wordplayers like to do is create new words by blending two existing words. Sometimes these become popular and enter into everyday language, like sitcom (situation + comedy) and chortle (chuckle + snort). Can you work out where these came from?

Answers on page 157.

- brunch
- infotainment
- labradoodle
- vlog
- spork
- mockumentary
- carjack
- Bollywood

- chillax
- vomitrocious
- chunnel
- swapportunity
- fantabulous
- manbag
- ginormous
- guesstimate

12 Expressions from Shakespeare

William Shakespeare was an ace inventor of memorable phrases – all of these are still used 400 years after he croaked:

Salad days (Anthony and Cleopatra)

Cruel to be kind (Hamlet)

Eaten me out of house and home (Henry V Part 2)

The dogs of war (Julius Caesar)

What's in a name? (Romeo and Juliet)

For ever and a day (As You Like It)

A laughing stock (Merry Wives of Windsor)

Good riddance (Troilus and Cressida)

In a pickle (The Tempest)

Lie low (Much Ado About Nothing)

Mum's the word (Henry VI Part 2)

Thereby hangs a tale (As You Like It)

Double dictionary

Wordplayers from the past have created many memorable additions to the dictionary using the word double:

DOUBLE ACT two people performing together, for example Laurel and Hardy.

DOUBLE AGENT a cheeky spy who spies for the country he's pretending to spy on.

DOUBLE BOGEY not a twin-nostril snot-shocker but a score of two over par in golf.

DOUBLE-CROSS to trick or betray a person who trusted you: naughty!

DOUBLE-DECKER a bus with two levels, beloved of London.

DOUBLE DUTCH language that makes no sense at all: gibberish!

DOUBLE FAULT two consecutive service boo-boos in tennis.

DOUBLE JOINTED being able to flex your body in unusual ways.

DOUBLE NEGATIVE a kind of mangled talk, for example, 'I aint got nothing.'

DOUBLESPEAK when something is said to deliberately confuse the listener.

DOUBLE TAKE when you suddenly notice something a moment after it happened.

DOUBLE TROUBLE er, more trouble than expected, really.

DOUBLE WHAMMY a setback on top of another setback. Bad.

Daffynitions

A definition is the meaning of a word. A daffynition is a silly meaning of the word based on a pun or simply what it sounds like. See if you can work out these:

CROSSBAR ⟶ an angry pub

PALETTE ⟶ a small friend

MARITIME ⟶ when the wedding starts

LAVISH ⟶ like a toilet

HURRICANE ⟶ a stick for helping you walk fast

MANGLE ⟶ male seabird

RELIEF ⟶ what trees do in spring

LENS ⟶ belonging to Len

BUSKING ⟶ the head of Transport for London

CARTON ⟶ 100 mph

BLOCKADE ⟶ fizzy drink made from bricks

SPECTACULAR ⟶ short-sighted vampire

CHECKMATE ⟶ see if your friend is OK

BUOYANT ⟶ male insect

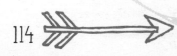

RAQs

These Rarely Asked Questions are not meant to be answered
– they are just another witty form of wordplay.

Why is it that night falls but day breaks?

Why is the time of day with the slowest traffic called rush hour?

Is it good if a vacuum cleaner really sucks?

Why when I buy a pair of knickers do I only get one?

If people from Poland are called Poles, why aren't people from Holland called Holes?

Are you telling the truth if you lie in bed?

If vegetable oil is made from vegetables what is baby oil made from?

Why do people tell you when they are speechless?

If an orange is orange, why isn't a lemon called a yellow?

What happens if you go on a survival course and you don't pass?

Why is your bottom in your middle?

What if the hokey cokey really is what it's all about?

Rubbish anagrams

Anagrams are word puzzles where you need to rearrange the letters to find something familiar. Work these out (some of them are not hard!) then try to think of some of your own:

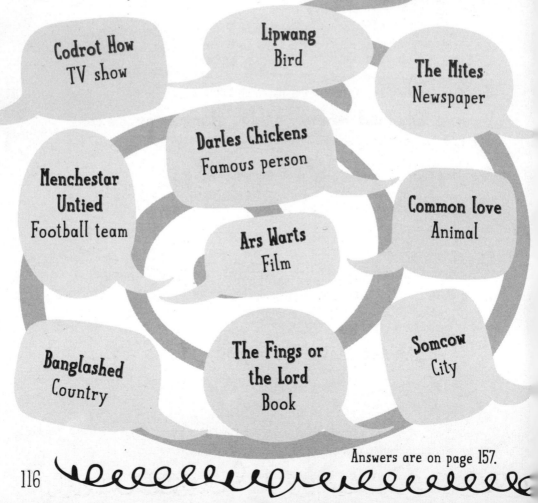

Codrot How
TV show

Lipwang
Bird

The Mites
Newspaper

Darles Chickens
Famous person

Menchestar Untied
Football team

Ars Warts
Film

Common love
Animal

Banglashed
Country

The Fings or the Lord
Book

Somcow
City

Answers are on page 157.

Suspect sentences

Sometimes, quite by accident, people write things which have a double meaning. Sometimes the meaning they didn't mean (if you know what I mean) produces something funny. Can you find the double meaning in the sentences below?

Jenny accidentally hit the man with the sandwich.

While she was waiting Zac gave her cat food.

I met a woman in a wheelchair called Hilda.

Groucho saw an elephant in his pyjamas.

The dog chased the boy on a skateboard.

If you don't get these look on page 158.

Paraprosdokians

A paraprosdokian is a sentence or quote which takes you by the surprise because of its unexpected ending. Some are clever and some are funny...

Change is inevitable... except from a vending machine.

'If I am reading this graph correctly—I'd be very surprised.'
Stephen Colbert

'If all the people who fell asleep in church on Sunday morning were laid out end to end they would be a great deal more comfortable.'
Abraham Lincoln

'If I could just say a few words...I'd be a better public speaker.'
Homer Simpson

'I've had a perfectly wonderful evening, but this wasn't it.'
Groucho Marx

Some cause happiness wherever they go. Others, whenever they go.

'Before you criticize a man, walk a mile in his shoes. That way, you will be a mile away and he won't have any shoes.'

There's nothing like a good pie— and this is nothing like a good pie.

'I haven't slept for ten days, because that would be too long.'
Mitch Hedberg

Abbreviation variation

English is full of abbreviations and acronyms like BBC, NATO and DVD and it's useful to know what they stand for. But it's also a lot of fun to pretend they stand for something else:

Abbreviation	Stands for	Doesn't stand for	Definitely doesn't stand for
IOU	I owe you	Ian's on Uranus	Is oozing unacceptable?
BTW	By the way	Bought two wombats	Babysitters talk Welsh
VAT	Value Added Tax	Voles are trouble	Very annoying teabag
RSVP	répondez s'il vous plaît (please reply)	Really silly vegetable pizza	Rachel sometimes vaults peaches
CIA	Central Intelligence Agency	Clucked in anger	Custard is awesome
FAQ	Frequently Asked Questions	Frogs annoy Queen	Fiona apparently quacks
UNICEF	United Nations International Children's Emergency Fund	Usually Norman is crooning every Friday	Unless necessary I can't eat floorboards

Gibberish

Gibberish means a nonsensical language but it's also the name of a word game played around the world. It works by adding groups of letters such as 'idig' to ordinary words to change them, for example:

cat > **cidigat**

show > **shidigow**

out > **idigout**

brother > **bridigothidiger**

Other groups of letters can be used such as uvug, atheb, op, iz and uz.

Ubbi Dubbi

Ubbi Dubbi is a gibberish game which became popular in the USA for a time. It works by adding 'ub' before each vowel in a word to create a new nonsense language. Here are some examples:

yes > **yubes**

hello > **hubellubo**

fantastic > **fubantubastubic**

what's going on? > **Whubat's guboubing ubon?**

Ubbi Dubbi > **Ububbubi Dububbubi**

Crubazy stubuff ubisn't ubit?

Pig Latin

Pig Latin is another wordplay language where each word is changed by following two simple rules.

Rule 1
(for words beginning with consonants):

Move the first consonant(s) to the end of the word

Add 'ay' onto the end

Examples:

dog > ogday

sheep > eepshay

computer > omputercay

Rule 2
(for words beginning with vowels):

Just add 'ay' to the end

Examples:

at > atay

egg > eggay

international > internationalay

Pig Latin can be used to keep a message hidden from people who don't know how it works. Can you de-code this?

igpay atinlay ashay eaturedfay inay ooksbay, ilmsfay, ongssay, advertsay anday VTay owsshay ikelay ethay impsonssay.

(Answer on page 158.)

Other sneaky languages

As well as Gibberish, Ubbi Dubbi and Pig Latin, there are many other coded languages used to disguise messages from listeners. These include:

Alibi

Used by children in Australia and New Zealand. It works by repeating vowel sounds and adding the letters l and b in between the extra vowels.
Example: hello > helebel-lolobo

Double Dutch

Also called Tutnese, this secret language is more complicated than most. It involves replacing every consonant in a word with a new syllable: B is replaced with bub; W is replaced with wack and so on.
Example: cat > cashatut

Back slang

From England, this code works by saying words backwards by sound. It was often used in the past by butchers and market traders to keep information from customers. The word 'yob' (boy) developed from this.
Example: table > eltab

Dog Latin

Like Pig Latin but without the rules, this is more of a comedy version of Latin with spoof words simply created to sound like proper Latin.
Example: big shark > sharkus maximus

Nonsense-shmonsense!

A popular form of verbal wit in America is called 'shm reduplication'. It involves repeating a word with shm replacing the beginning (e.g. 'coffee-shmoffee'). It's usually used during a conversation to dismiss an idea in a humorous way.

Examples:

 Mo: That pudding was not too bad.

Flo: **Pudding-shmudding! It tasted like toe medicine.**

 Lou: This shirt was a bargain.

Pru: **Bargain-shmargain – you were swindled!**

'Shm' is also sometimes spelt 'schm':

apple – schmapple

walk – schmalk

Blue Peter – Blue Schmeter

Pirates of the Caribbean – Pirates of the Schmaribbean.

In the USA, the name for a typical/ordinary person ('Joe Bloggs' in the UK) is Joe-Shmoe.

Mondo mondegreens

Mondegreens are misheard words from songs, poems, etc. Here are some amusing samples:

Source	Actual words	Heard as
Carol: The First Noel	Born is the King of Israel	Barney's the king of Israel
Carol: God Rest ye Merry Gentlemen	God rest ye, merry gentlemen	Get dressed ye married gentlemen,
BBC radio programme title	Crossing Continents	Cross incontinents
Psalm 23 from the Bible	Surely goodness and mercy shall follow me all the days of my life	Surely Good Mrs Murphy shall follow me all the days of my life
Carol: Hark! The Herald Angels Sing	Joyful all ye nations rise	Joyful oily nations rise
Carol: Away in a Manger	The cattle are lowing	The catalogue glowing
Song: The Twelve Days of Christmas	On the twelfth day of Christmas, My true love sent to me	On the twelfth day of Christmas, My tulip sent to me

Peculiar palindromes

Palindomes are words, phrases or sentences that read the same backwards. Simple examples are words like pip and level or names like Bob and Hannah. Some wordplayers take great delight in making the longest palindrome sentences they can, although these often do end up sounding like twaddle!

Examples of palindromes:

Wet stew.

Never odd or even.

'Madam, I'm Adam.'

A Toyota's a Toyota.

Rats live on no evil star.

'Was it Eliot's toilet I saw?'

A man, a plan, a canal: Panama.

'Was it a car or a cat I saw?'

'Anne, I vote more cars race Rome to Vienna.'

Challenge: can you make up a palindrome?

Looney Tunes catchphrases

In the golden age of hand-drawn animation, Warners Bros studio in America produced a classic series of short cartoons called Looney Tunes, featuring these characters and their celebrated catchphrases:

Name	Catchphrase
Bugs Bunny	'What's up doc?'
Daffy Duck	'You're dethpicable!'
Road Runner	'Beep beep!'
Wile E. Coyote	(Never speaks)
Sylvester	'Sufferin' succotash!'
Porky Pig	'That's all folks!'
Elmer Fudd	'You wascally wabbit!'
Tweety Pie	'I tawt I taw a puddy tat.'

Haven't a clue?

The BBC Radio comedy panel show I'm Sorry I Haven't a Clue has been running for over 40 years and is famous for its clever and silly wordplay. In one game, the panellists are given a title then come up with witty examples, often based on puns. Here are two examples of their humour:

Film prequels

A sequel is a film that follows on from another film and a prequel comes before another film. The team thought up these comedy prequels for classic films:

FILM*	PREQUEL
Forrest Gump	Sapling Gump
The Empire Strikes Back	The Empire Gets Hit
Gulliver's Travels	Gulliver's Packing
Carry On Camping	Begin Camping
King Kong	Prince Kong

*You may need to wait until you are older before watching some of these films.

Budget TV

These are silly versions of TV shows and movies, made on the cheap – the real versions are in brackets:

Alice in Poundland
(Alice in Wonderland)

Thomas The Tank Top
(Thomas the Tank Engine)

Star Truck (Star Trek)

Charlie And The Chocolate Biscuit
(Charlie and the Chocolate Factory)

Joseph And His Amazing Beige Cardigan
(Joseph And His Amazing Technicolour Dreamcoat)

Can you think of some more for each list?

Just nutty

A mishmash of bits 'n' bobs, odds and ends, this and that, scraps and sundries – all fooling around with words.

Rivals to Meals on Wheels

Snacks on tracks

Snails on rails

Hams on prams

Colas on rollers

Dates on skates

Oats on boats

Peas on skis

Bum deals

BOGOF: 'Buy one get one free' is a good deal — these are not:

Buy one get none free

Buy two get one broken

Buy one get one flea

Buy one get lost

Buy 754 get one free

Who rules OK?

☞ Boxing rules KO
☞ Town criers rule OK, OK, OK
☞ Queen Elizabeth rules UK
☞ Cowards rule, if that's OK with you
☞ James Bond rules OOK
☞ Amnesia rules O
☞ Matadors rule Olé

If the only vowel was O...

This is how you'd count to ten....

- ono
- two
- throo
- foor
- fovo
- sox
- sovon
- ooght
- nono
- ton

...and these would be some names of things:

Newspaper:
Dooly Mool

Rapper:
Ononom

Our Monarch:
Tho Quoon

Clothing:
Too short

Baby's game:
Poopo

Country:
Spoon

3.142
Po

Meal:
Poo & hom soop

School subject:
Moths

Colour:
Ponk

TV Show:
Bog Brothor

Nursery Rhyme:
Lottlo Bo Poop

Waki wikis

Wikipedia is the largest and most popular online encyclopedia. But what if it were split up into smaller sections? Here are a few silly ideas (these are fun to guess):

An online encyclopedia of...

→ Biscuits: **Bikipedia**

   → Magic: **Trikipedia**

→ Hens: **Chikipedia**

    → Websites: **Clikipedia**

→ Speed: **Quikipedia**

→ Disney: **Mikipedia**

→ Football: **Kikipedia**

→ Clocks: **Tikipedia**

→ Walls **Brikipedia**

→ Glue: **Stikipedia**

→ Illnesses: **Sikipedia**

Blend-a-book

There are many classic children's books around but what would happen if some of them were merged? This!

Wind in the Willows + **The Lion, the Witch and the Wardrobe**

= Wind in the Wardrobe

Anne of Green Gables + **Charlie and the Chocolate Factory**

= Anne of Green Chocolate

Peter Pan + **Winnie the Pooh**

= Peter Pooh

A Journey to the Centre of the Earth + **Cat in the Hat**

= Journey to the Centre of the Hat

James and the Giant Peach + **Little Women**

= James and the Giant Women

20,000 Leagues Under the Sea + **The Secret Garden**

= 20,000 Leagues under the Garden

Can you come up with better blends? Here are a few more classic titles you could use:

⊙ **Alice's Adventures in Wonderland**   ⊙ Swallows and Amazons

⊙ The Call of the Wild   ⊙ **The Jungle Book**

⊙ **Charlotte's Web**   ⊙ Black Beauty

⊙ The Railway Children   ⊙ **Rip Van Winkle**

WACKY WORD GAMES

The best wordplay is often that which you make up yourself. Here are all sorts of ideas for games, activities, challenges, puzzles and fun things to do with words. Some of them don't need anything at all but most require a pen and paper.

Yabber yabber

You need at least two people for this. Players take turns to say words from a chosen category, working through the alphabet starting with A, B, C and so on until they are stuck.

Example (using the category FRUIT & VEG, with 3 players)

Player 1 says: **apple**
Player 2 says: **avocado**
Player 3 is stuck, so move on to the letter B with player 2 starting this time.
Player 2 says: **banana**
Player 3 says: **broccoli**
Player 1 says: **beans**
Player 2 is stuck, so move on to the letter C with player 3 starting, and so on

Variations

Each player can have 3 lives and
anyone who loses 3 lives is out.
Keep a score and whoever says the
most examples by the letter Z wins.

Categories

Choose one of these categories to play with or make up your own:

Girls' names/boys' names
Animals
Foods
Sports
TV programmes

Books
Films
Songs
Parts of the body
Gadgets/inventions

Football teams
Toys
Sweets/chocolate bars
Famous people (surnames)

Never-ending sentence

This needs at least two people. Players take turns to add words to a sentence, trying not to end it. The sentence can be about anything and the crazier it is, the more fun the game is (although the sentence does have to make sense from a grammatical point of view).

Example (with four players)

Player 1 says: **There**

Player 2 says: **once**

Player 3 says: **were**

Player 4 says: **seven**

Player 1 says: **pizzas**

Player 2 says: **flying**

Player 3 says: **through**

Player 4 says: **a**

Player 1 says: **huge**

Player 2 says: **hotel**

Player 3 says: **which**

Player 4 says: **had**

(and so on)

Variations

✪ You can choose a subject for your sentence (for example a person, an object, a food, an idea) or it can just be random.

◉ Whoever ends the sentence or is stuck can be out.

✪ Try going quickly.

◉ For a really tricky challenge, all the words must start with a chosen letter such as P.

Nuttinitials

This is a very simple speaking game based on the initials of people's names. To play you simply give people silly descriptions using the letters of their initials. Rude or nasty names are not allowed.
It can be played using people you know or with celebrities.

Examples:

Megan Jones — massages jellyfish

Nasir Kiran — never knits

Charlie Oliver Benson — can't open bananas

Emma Watson — enjoys whistling

David Beckham — doesn't busk

Peppa Pig — pink poppet

Doctor Who — Daleks worry

Variations:

*Try fictional people as well as real people

*Use middle names as well

*With friends, each write a list then read out your three best

*Do categories such as singers, cartoon characters, TV presenters

*Rather than silly descriptions try to make ones which are true, for example:

Usain Bolt — unusually brisk

Scooby Doo — scaredy dog

Queen Victoria — quietly veiled

Endy

This an easy speaking game that works with groups of two or more. You simply pick a subject, such as birds, and then each person says an example. Each word must begin with the last letter of the previous word, so if the first person says 'robin', the next bird must begin with N.

Example:

Person 1 says: **starling**
Person 2 says: **gannet**
Person 3 says: **thrush**
Person 1 says: **harris hawk**
Person 2 says: **kingfisher**
Person 3 says: **reed warbler**
And so on.

Categories

It's best to choose a category that has lots of possible examples such as:
Foods
Animals
Girls' names or boys' names
Objects found in a house

If you are good at it, try some harder categories such as countries, famous people (surnames), songs, towns/cities or sports.

Variations:

Each person has three lives. Anyone who is stuck loses a life and is out when they lose all three lives.
For an easier version the next word can begin with any letter in the previous example.
If you're on your own you can try a similar pen and paper alphabet challenge: write down a word that begins with A and ends with B. The next word must begin with B and end in C and so on. See how far you can get, for example:

Absorb ＞ bloc ＞

called ＞ doze

Road sign countdown

This is a good game to play when on a car journey — it's based on the TV show Countdown. Pick a place name from a road sign and see who can make the longest word using the letters in it. It's best to avoid places with very short or very long names.

Example:
Using the place name Glasgow
Player 1 says: slow (4 letters)
Player 2 says: wag (3 letters)
Player 3 says: glows (5 letters)
Player 3 wins

Example:
Using the place name Cambridge
Player 1 says: ridge (5)
Player 2 says: bridge (6)
Player 3 says: birdcage (8)
Player 3 wins

Variations:

Look out for funny place names and give them made-up meanings, for example:

Borth — a seashore rock covered in slime

Molash — dropped food

Siddick — a small stone in your shoe that won't come out.

Change one letter on a road sign to make it funnier, for example:

Liverpool › **Loverpool**

Belfast › **Welfast**

Clacton-on-Sea › **Clacton-on-Tea**

Watford › **Watfor?**

Blackburn › **Blackburp**

Alpha me

This is a memory game as much as a wordplay game but opportunity to have fun with words too. It's also very si number can join in.

The first person says, 'A is for ___' (something beginning next person repeats this followed by, 'B is for _____' (sc with B). The third person repeats each of the first two li C. Anything can be chosen beginning with the given lett ... uoes not have to be a single word. You are out if you can't remember all the words and the last person in is the winner.

Example:

Player 1 says: A is for armpit.

Player 2 says: A is for armpit and B is for broken wafers.

Player 3 says: A is for armpit and B is for broken wafers and C is for California.

Player 1 says: A is for armpit and B is for broken wafers and C is for California and D is for Derek Jones.

Player 2 can't remember what C was for, so is out.

(And so on).

Variations:

To make it easier, you can stick to one word for each letter.

You can give the game a theme, for example every word could be a fruit or vegetable. Other themes could be: animals, places, parts of the body, people or toys/games.

The letters K, Q and X are often very difficult (or even impossible if you are following a theme) so you can make up words for those or miss them out.

minister's cat

er alphabet game but it's not a memory game.
hat each person comes up with a word to
minister's cat (which can be any kind of
e). The first person says a describing word
ning with A, the second person says one starting with B and so on.

Variations:

Traditionally this game is played to a clapping beat to make it more challenging and fun. To do this everyone claps four times in between each person speaking – the rhythm should match a typical slow counting pace: one-two-three-four.

Instead of the minister's cat, create your own animal and owner. Or you can make up a fictional person and describe him or her: Beverley Ross is an artistic girl; Beverley Ross is a bossy girl and so on.

Example:

Player 1 says: The minister's cat is an angry cat. (letter A)
Player 2 says: The minister's cat is a beautiful cat. (letter B)
Player 3 says: The minister's cat is a crafty cat. (letter C)
Player 4 says: The minister's cat is a damp cat. (letter D)
Player 1 says: The minister's cat is an educated cat. (letter E)
And so on.

I don't spy

Everyone knows how to play I Spy but have you ever played this much wackier version? The person whose turn it is thinks of something they can't see and everyone has to guess what it is. The crazier the better!

Example:

Person 1 says: I don't spy with my big eye something beginning with C
Person 2 says: Christopher Columbus? [No]
Person 3 says: Cornwall? [No]
Person 2 says: a concrete banana? [No]
Person 3 says: camel curry? [No]

After a while they give up and the answer is revealed to be cheese on toast.

Variations:

● The person whose turn it is must give a clue after each guess.

● If the item has more than one word then this can be given at the start, so in the above example Person 1 would say 'something beginning with C-O-T'. The guesses must then match these letters:

• Cup of tea? • A computer of tomorrow? •
• Crusty old trumpets? • Crying otter trouble? •

In with the new

It's fun to give meanings to made-up words. What do you think these mean?

kurf • smollop • yagnig • conboomerate • primpo • hax

Make up some new words to match these meanings:

An itch you can't reach.

The sound of a heavy book landing on a table.

When water comes too fast out of a tap.

A hanging thread of spider's web covered in dust.

A person who takes up two seats on a train.

The little broken bits of crisps at the bottom of the bag.

Variations:

▷ Make up your own new words – a good way to do this is to blend two existing words (remember to give your new words a meaning).

▷ Take a word and change it by one letter. Then change another letter. Keep doing this until you have a brand new word with completely different letters.

▷ Pick your three favourite and least favourite words and say why you like/hate them.

Adder

Adder involves making words by adding one letter at a time, in turns. Any number can play. The idea is to keep going for as long as possible by adding a letter to any part of the word. The best way to understand this is with some examples:

Example A:
Player 1 says: i (you can start with any letter of the alphabet)
Player 2 says: in (adding n)
Player 1 says: pin (adding p)
Player 2 says: spin (adding s)
Player 1 says: spins (adding s)
Player 2 says: spines (adding e)
Player 1 cannot add another letter to make a word so player 2 wins

Example B:
Player 1 says: t
Player 2 says: at
Player 1 says: ant
Player 2 says: want
Player 1 says: wants
Player 2 cannot add another letter to make a word so player 1 wins

Variations:
You can play reverse adder where you start with a word and take away letters to make new words. The person who starts must be able to make a make a new word (by taking away one letter) if challenged or he/she loses. Example: tables > table > able > ale
The game on the next page, Ghost, is very similar

Ghost

Ghost is like Adder on the previous page but this time you are trying not to finish a word when you add a letter to a letter string – you just have to prove that your letter string is part of a longer word. Sounds complicated? These examples will make it clear:

Example A:

Player 1 says: o
Player 2 says: oc
Player 3 says: ock
Player 1 says: ockw
Player 2 doesn't think Player 4 can make a word with those letters so challenges her. Player 1 says her word was 'clockwork' so Player 1 wins. A player can challenge the player that goes before him or her

Example B:

Player 2 says: v (a different player should start each time)
Player 3 says: ev
Player 1 says: eve
Player 1 has finished a word ('eve') and so has lost this time. Player 3 wins because he made the last letter string.

Example C:

Player 3 says: s
Player 1 says: sm
Player 2 says: sem
Player 3 says: selm
Player 1 doesn't think Player 3 can make a word with those letters so challenges him. Player 3 can't think of a word containing 'selm' so he loses and Player 1 wins for making a correct challenge.

Games in brief: talking

Here is a selection of further word games to try:

Interrogation

For two or more players. One player is the suspect and the others are detectives questioning him/her. The suspect can only answer with a single word each time and all the answers begin with the same letter. Begin by choosing the letter. If the suspect gets stuck, swap roles and letters.

Questions, questions...

A tricky game for older players but good fun. Two people take part and have a conversation, but they can only speak in questions! First one to go wrong loses. For example:

A: Are you OK?
B: Why do you ask?
A: It's not a problem, is it?
B: Have we met before?

A-Z Conversation

For two or more people. One person starts a conversation saying something beginning with A. The next person must continue starting with B and so on. For example:

A: Are any of you going out later?
B: Billy is I think.
C: Can't I go?
A: Don't be ridiculous, you're too young.

Consequences

You need two people for this silly traditional writing game (which is a lot of fun). Each person needs a piece of paper and a pen.

1 Fold each piece of paper in half then in half again the same way then in half once more. Open it out – it should be divided into 8 sections like this:

2 In the first section at the top, each player writes the name of a male person. It can be anyone at all, real or fictional, dead or alive. Celebrities are good to use, as are friends and family. Fold this section back so it cannot be seen.

3 In the second section write 'met'. Fold this back then swap the papers.

4 In the next empty section write the name of a female person – anyone you like, young or old. Fold this section back so it cannot be seen.

5 In the next empty section write the word 'at'. Fold this back then swap the papers.

6 In the next blank section write the name of a place. It can be anywhere at all: a building, a shop, on top of a mountain, someone's house, inside a box, on a vehicle or ship, abroad, even in space!

7 Fold this back and swap the papers.

8 In the next section write 'He said' followed by a quote – a short piece of speech said by the male person. It can be anything at all. You can use speech marks. Fold this back and swap the papers.

9 In the next section write 'She said' and write something funny that the female character might say. Swap the papers again.

10 You should just have the last empty section left. In this you write what happened: some kind of event. Often it begins with, 'They...' but it does not need to – it can be anything at all. When you have both finished, swap the papers for the last time then read them aloud.

Example

Mickey Mouse met The Queen at Tesco's bakery. He said, 'My toe just fell off.' She said, 'Booyah!' They went to Peebles.

Ognib

Ognib is bingo backwards and it's a game that needs at least three people. Each person needs a pen and a piece of paper. The game involves one person calling out letters of the alphabet and the other people trying to make words from them to fit a given category.

How to play

1. The caller is chosen. He or she writes the 26 letters of the alphabet on a piece of paper.

2. The caller also chooses a category for the other players: this should be something easy like animals, girls' names, or food. Other categories to try are towns/cities, birds, household objects and parts of the body.

3. The caller calls out random letters from the alphabet one at a time (with several seconds in between) and crosses them off his/her list. The players write them down.

4. The players have to make a word from the given letters as soon as they can. As soon as they have got a word that fits they shout 'ognib!' and the caller checks if it's right. If it is that person wins the round.

Example:

The chosen category is animals.
The caller calls out Z, T, A, V, L, U, B
Player 2 spots 'bat' so calls out 'Ognib!'
It is correct so player 2 gets one point.
Everyone crosses out those letters.
The caller calls out E, R, K, X, C, O
Player 1 spots 'ox' so calls out 'Ognib!' She gets a point.
The game continues until all of the letters are used. A different person then takes over as caller with a new alphabet.

Variations:

1. You can have more one category running at a time – for example you could have animals and foods. The winner would be the first person to find an example of both things.

2. Instead of shouting 'Ognib' after one example has been found, you can let the caller get to the end of the alphabet then count up how many examples you found.

Listo

This is another old favourite. Any number can play and everyone needs some lined paper and a pen. It's also useful to have a ruler. The idea is to write down as many examples of things as you can, one for each letter of the alphabet.

How to play

1 Start by writing the alphabet down the margin on the left of the page.

2 Decide how many categories you are going to have. It can be one, two or more. The categories need to be subjects with lots of examples, eg:

Animals

Countries

Colours

Boys' names

Girls' names

Foods

Famous people (surnames)

Towns and cities

Pop groups or singers

Sports

Vehicles

3 Write the title of each chosen category at the top of the page like this

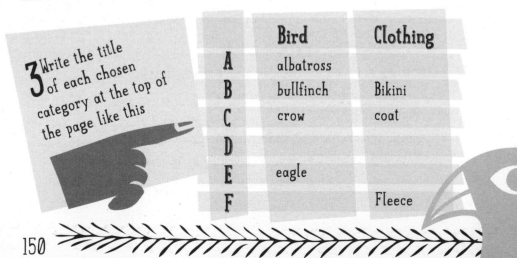

	Bird	Clothing
A	albatross	
B	bullfinch	Bikini
C	crow	coat
D		
E	eagle	
F		Fleece

4 When everyone is ready, say 'go' and then fill in as many sections as you can with each word beginning with each letter of the alphabet. Try and think of unusual answers.

5 You can say stop after a certain time (such as 15 minutes) or you can stop when everyone is stuck or one person has finished. You may want to leave out the letter X (or even Q and Z as well!)

6 For the first category, everybody reads out their answer for each letter. You only get a point if you have a word that no one else has got. The winner is the person with the most points for each category.

Variations:

Think up some wacky categories such as funny words or things that don't go in sandwiches.

Words that begin and end with the same letter or contain a double letter (aa, bb etc) is a good challenge for older players

Namegame

This is very much like nuttinitials, above, but it uses whole names and so needs to be written down. To play you write down a person's name (either first name or surname) then make a phrase or sentence from the letters, as below.

Examples:

ANDREW: Always needs dry rhubarb every week

CHLOE: Can't help leaping on elks

HUSSAIN: His underpants suggest something alarming in Nottingham

MR JONES: My raspberry jelly occasionally needs extra shaking

Variations:

You can try and make the sentence/phrase into a description of the person. Try this for famous people or historical figures.

Namegame also works for places such as towns, or football clubs or shops or all sorts of things!

More writing games

Here are some other games to try – you'll need a pen and paper (or you can use the empty pages at the back of the book).

Title Shocker

Each person copies down a headline from a newspaper. You are allowed to change four letters in the headline to change its meaning. Read them out and decide whose is best.

This also works well for long titles of books, films, TV shows etc.

Word Killer

For any number of players. This game is like the old favourite Battleships. Each person writes the alphabet and a five letter word underneath, keeping it secret. The players then take turns to say one letter that isn't in their word (cross it off the alphabet when you say it). If the letter is in anyone's word they must cross it out. Keep saying letters until someone's word is 'dead' and they are out. The winner is the last one with letters left in their word.

Grimericks

For older players (who know how limericks work). It's best played with 4-6 people. First, a theme is chosen, which can be anything at all. Next, each person writes the first line of a limerick. Each paper is then passed on to the left and everyone writes the second line of the limerick they are given. This continues, so that every poem is passed on and everyone contributes at least one line to each one. At the end, read them out for some entertainment.

Jumblets

How many words (of 3 or more letters) can you make using the letters in each of these puzzles? Names are not allowed. Can you find the six-letter word each time? Answers on page 158.

D	E	P
L	A	D

V	R	I
S	L	E

U	B	H
O	T	G

1. Target: 12 words.

2. Target: 10 words.

3. Target: 15 words.

Modify your mates

How can you make Jake edible? By changing one letter so he becomes cake! See if you can change one letter in each name to solve the puzzle.
Answers on page 158.

☞ Make Bill ring
Make Leah jump
Make Kate rush
Make Miles creamy

☞ Make Lucy fortunate
Make Noah surprised
Make Grace fruity
Make Matt shipshape

Crackit?

Can you crack these codes and discover what the messages are?
Warning: some of them are tricky!
Answers on page 159.

1. Therearenowordsthatrhymewiththewordwolfhoweverhardyoutry

2. Of yoo con got thos yoo oro vory clover

3. O I C U R A DJ 2

4. yram dah a elttil bmal, sti eceelf saw etihw sa wons

5. Take that bread and get some rosy from down the frog

6. ric char dofy orkga veb att leinva in

7. iijt dpef jt b cju ibsefs
   iibo uif uxp bcpwf

8. tcroy dteos moafkye
   ouupr soowmne

ANSWERS

Jokes and Riddles

Riddles to untwiddle (page 12)

1. A cold.
2. A bottle
3. A clock.
4. Your breath.
5. An egg.
6. The word wholesome.
7. A palm.
8. Short.

Brain-ache riddles (page 13)

1. A teapot.
2. A pillow.
3. A stamp.
4. Silence.
5. A candle.
6. A river.
7. Your mind.
8. Adverbs (each word is or can be an adverb).

Nutty riddles (page 14)

1. Envelope.
2. Edam.
3. The C.
4. The Post Office.
5. A ton.
6. A coat of paint.
7. Today and tomorrow.
8. Four.
9. In the dictionary.
10. Dead.

Spoonerisms

Quoonerism Spiz (page 69)

1. Jelly beans
2. Bad manners
3. Flat battery
4. I took a shower
5. Pack of lies
6. Funny bone
7. Healing the sick
8. Four of diamonds
9. Lighting a fire
10. Smart fella

Miscellaneous malarkey

Proverbial pandemonium

(page 110)

A bird in the hand is worth two in the bush.

Blood is thicker than water.

Boys will be boys.

Curiosity killed the cat.

Don't put all your eggs in one basket.

In for a penny, in for a pound.

It's no use crying over spilt milk.

It takes two to tango.

Look before you leap.

Never look a gift horse in the mouth.

Prevention is better than cure.

Too many cooks spoil the broth.

Two heads are better than one.

Two wrongs do not make a right.

Walls have ears.

Portmanteau creations

(page 111)

Brunch: breakfast and lunch

Infotainment: information and entertainment

Labradoodle: labrador and poodle

Vlog: video and blog

Spork: spoon and fork

Mockumentary: mock and documentary

Carjack: car and hijack

Bollywood: Bombay and Hollywood

Chillax: chill out and relax

Vomitrocious: vomit and atrocious

Chunnel: channel and tunnel

Swapportunity: swap and opportunity

Fantabulous: fantastic and fabulous

Manbag: man and handbag

Ginormous: giant and enormous

Guesstimate: guess and estimate

Rubbish anagrams (page 116)

Darles Chickens = Charles Dickens

Common love = Common vole

Lipwang = lapwing

Banglashed = Bangladesh

Menchestar Untied = Manchester United

Somcow = Moscow

The Mites = The Times

The Fings or the Lord = The Lord of the Rings

Codrot How = Doctor Who

Ars Warts = Star Wars

Suspect Sentences (page 117)

Did Jenny use a sandwich to hit a man, or did she hit a man who was holding a sandwich?

Did Zac feed her cat, or did Zac feed her?

Was the wheelchair called Hilda, or was the woman called Hilda?

Was Groucho wearing pyjamas when he saw the elephant, or was the elephant wearing pyjamas?

Was the dog on a skateboard, or was the boy on the skateboard?

Pig Latin (page 121)

Pig Latin has featured in books, films, songs, adverts and TV shows like The Simpsons.

Word Games

Jumblets (page 154)

1. The six-letter word is **PADDLE**. You can also have: pad, pal, pale, pea, peal, plea, pedal, plead, add, ale, ape, dale, deal, dad, dead, lap, lad, ladle, lea, lead, leap (there are other harder words too!)

2. The six letter word is **SILVER** or **LIVERS** or **SLIVER**. You can also have: sir, sire, ire, live, lie, lies, lives, liver, vie, vile, viler, rile, riles, rev, revs, rise (there are other harder words too!)

3. The six-letter word is **BOUGHT**. You can also have: bog, bot, bug, but, bout, both, ought, out, ugh, gob, got, goth, gout, hob, hub, hog, hot, hug, tog, tug, tub, thug, thou (there are other harder words too!)

Modify your mates (page 154)

1. Bell
2. Leap
3. Late
4. Milks
5. Luck

6. Woah
7. **Grape**
8. Mast

Crackit? (page 155)

1. There are no words that rhyme with the word wolf however hard you try [the spaces were taken out]

2. **If you can get this you are very clever** [all vowels changed to 'o']

3. Oh, I see you are a deejay too. [Uses sounds of letters and numbers]

4. **Mary had a little lamb, its fleece was white as snow** [the words were written backwards]

5. Take that money and get some tea from down the road [Uses rhyming slang: bread and honey = money, rosy lea = tea; frog and toad = road]

6. **Richard of York gave battle in vain** [the spaces between the words have been moved]

7. This code is a bit harder than the two above [each letter is swapped for the one after it in the alphabet, so a>b, b>c, s>t, t>u etc.]

8. **Try to make up some codes of your own** [The sentence has been split into two halves and then the letters from each half have been merged together: tcroy dteo (read the bold letters then the other letters)]

FURTHER INFORMATION
Books to read

Here are some entertaining books if you enjoy playing with words:
Razzle Dazzle by Andy Seed(Hands Up Books, 2010)
Read Me and Laugh by Gaby Morgan (Macmillan, 2005)
The Ha Ha Bonk Book by Janet and Allan Ahlberg (Puffin, 1982)
Wicked Words by Terry Deary (Scholastic, 2011)
Phenomenal! The Small Book of Big Words by Jonathan Meres (Macmillan, 2011)

Websites

Jokes:
www.kidsjokes.co.uk/
www.ahajokes.com/kids_jokes.html

Poems:
http://childrenspoetryarchive.org/
http://poetryzone.co.uk/

Puzzles:
www.funenglishgames.com

ALSO AVAILABLE BY ANDY SEED:

£5.99

£5.99

The Silly Book ISBN 978-1-4088-5079-4,   The Anti-boredom Book ISBN 978-1-4088-5076-3]